ASIA PACIFIC SECURITY OUTLOOK 2001

The cosponsors of this project wish to thank

Asia Pacific Agenda Project

The Nippon Foundation

ASIA PACIFIC
SECURITY OUTLOOK
2001

edited by
Christopher A. McNally
and
Charles E. Morrison

cosponsored by

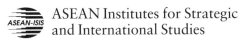 ASEAN Institutes for Strategic
and International Studies

East-West
Center

 Japan Center for
International Exchange

AN APAP PROJECT

Tokyo • Japan Center for International Exchange • *New York*

The surnames of the authors and other persons mentioned in this book are
positioned according to country practice.

Copyediting by Deborah Forbis and Pamela J. Noda.
Cover and typographic design by Becky Davis, EDS Inc., Editorial &
Design Services. Typesetting and production by EDS Inc.

Printed in Japan.
ISBN 4-88907-056-7

Distributed outside Japan by Brookings Institution Press (1775 Massachusetts
Avenue, N.W., Washington, D.C. 20036-2188 U.S.A.) and Kinokuniya
Company Ltd. (5-38-1 Sakuragaoka, Setagaya-ku, Tokyo 156-8691 Japan)

Japan Center for International Exchange
9-17 Minami Azabu 4-chome, Minato-ku, Tokyo 106-0047 Japan

URL: http://www.jcie.or.jp

Japan Center for International Exchange, Inc. (JCIE/USA)
1251 Avenue of the Americas, New York, N.Y. 10020 U.S.A.

Contents

Foreword

This is the fifth annual edition of the *Asia Pacific Security Outlook*, sponsored by the ASEAN Institutes for Strategic and International Studies, the East-West Center, and the Japan Center for International Exchange (JCIE).

The *Outlook* presents the distinctive national perspectives of most member countries of the ASEAN Regional Forum (ARF), based on background papers written in almost all cases by nationals of the country in question, in a form that facilitates comparison and the identification of areas where perceptions or interests differ. The objective is both to increase mutual understanding within the community of security analysts in the region and to help elucidate the key issues that will affect future regional security and stability.

Project participants mostly come from academic and research institutions in the member countries rather than from the government bureaucracies. Thus, the views expressed in the country chapters do not necessarily represent government views. However, the chapters are intended to present the mainstream points of view in the government and society of each country, as well as areas in which there are differences or unresolved issues in security policy.

We are pleased that Mongolia appears for the first time in this edition of the *Outlook*. With this addition, the series now includes 20 of the 23 ARF member countries, further progress toward the eventual goal of covering all ARF members.

We are grateful to all those who contributed to *Asia Pacific Security Outlook 2001*. The analysts and paper authors contributed both expertise and considerable time to the project. Professor Nishihara Masashi is a codirector of the *Outlook* project, along with Charles E. Morrison and Jusuf Wanandi. Christopher A. McNally of the East-West Center this year did the basic editing of the country chapters, working with coeditor Richard W. Baker and under the overall supervision of series editor Morrison. As in previous years, Wada Shūichi of JCIE coordinated the administrative aspects of the project. Clara Joewono of the Centre

7

for Strategic and International Studies of Jakarta handled the arrangements for the November 2000 project workshop, held in Bali, Indonesia, at which initial drafts of the papers were presented. Pamela J. Noda of JCIE again oversaw the copyediting and publication process.

The sponsoring institutions are grateful to the Nippon Foundation for its continuing financial support of the *Asia Pacific Security Outlook* as one element of the larger Asia Pacific Agenda Project, which is designed to promote policy-oriented intellectual dialogue among nongovernmental analysts in the Asia Pacific region.

CHARLES E. MORRISON
PRESIDENT
EAST-WEST CENTER

JUSUF WANANDI
FOUNDING MEMBER
ASEAN INSTITUTES FOR
STRATEGIC AND INTERNATIONAL STUDIES

YAMAMOTO TADASHI
PRESIDENT
JAPAN CENTER FOR INTERNATIONAL EXCHANGE

Regional Overview

In the preceding edition of this review, *Asia Pacific Security Outlook 2000*, the overall assessment of prospects for Asia Pacific security was pessimistic. It was pointed out then that widely held assumptions of the first post–cold war decade were being questioned in major countries. These included the perception that economic growth and interdependence were eroding political differences, that the nation-building process had been largely completed in the key states, and that both major states and regional institutions were contributing positively to security. However, countries were not in open conflict with each other, and security dialogue processes were continuing to expand.

The longer-term forecast continues to be mixed, but nearly all the analysts associated with *Asia Pacific Security Outlook 2001* believe that the region enters 2001 with a modestly more positive outlook. This is primarily due to several specific developments during 2000. The most dramatic was the opening in relations between North and South Korea sparked by the summit meeting between their leaders. While questions remain about the long-term impact of the meeting, the fact that it occurred and that the process of North-South dialogue continues has changed the entire tone of inter-Korean relations. There were also improvements in the relations between the larger powers, most importantly between China and the United States, whose relations had been damaged by the bombing of the Chinese Embassy in Belgrade. U.S.-Russian relations and Japanese-Russian relations also appear to have improved.

TROUBLING TRENDS

Still, there are troubling trends in the region that balance the positive developments. Four stand out.

DOMESTIC POLITICAL INSTABILITY   There is still a dangerous and unpredictable level of social and political instability in the region. Never in recent years have so many Asia Pacific leaders and governments experienced so much domestic political difficulty at the same time as at the beginning of 2001. The most significant problems exist in Indonesia, where real economic recovery is stalled, a high level of violence both in the provinces and in the capital continues, and a dangerously low and still declining degree of credibility for President Abdurrahman Wahid persists. At stake is the country's future that depends on its political system, its economy, its internal organization, its key institutions, and even its territorial reach. Because of its size, location, and resources, the outlook in Indonesia has implications for neighboring countries. The *Outlook* team identified instability in Indonesia as the most serious short-to-medium-term security issue facing the region.

The impeachment proceedings against President Joseph Estrada of the Philippines, accompanied by a resurgence of internal unrest in the southern islands and terrorist bombings in Manila, cast doubt on the future stability of that country also. The new year brought a dramatic conclusion to the presidential crisis, but through action in the streets rather than from constitutional processes. While the new leadership seemed likely to stabilize the country in the short term, the resolution of the crisis illustrated the weakness of the basic political and constitutional structure of the Philippines.

Political turmoil and violence were also affecting the fragile economies and polities of several Pacific Island nations—Fiji and the Solomon Islands—as well as Papua New Guinea.

The widespread political difficulties appear to have an underlying common pattern. They have been affecting mainly new democracies in societies that have never been fully integrated. Moreover, the inexorable forces of globalization are exacerbating the political pressures on all these new governments, making their democratic transitions even more treacherous. This dynamic promises to persist for as long as anyone can foresee.

ECONOMIC UNCERTAINTY   Except for Indonesia, developing East Asian economies made remarkably successful V-shaped recoveries in 1999 and early 2000. South Korea recovered its per capita gross domestic product of 1997 during 2000, and Thailand nearly did so. The strong economic performance considerably improved the security outlook during much of the past year.

However, the economic outlook is clouded by several factors. First, although much of the region managed economic recovery, it remains unclear whether a strong momentum toward new growth will materialize. Significant portions of the population in the region have been essentially left out of the recovery to date. The drive toward reforms that had appeared imperative during the crisis has stalled with recovery. In Thailand, Thaksin Shinawatra, now prime minister, emphasizes subsidies for villages and farmers and bailouts for business, not structural reforms. In South Korea, unions and owners combine to frustrate reform of the large, heavily indebted *chaebols*.

The generally poor political health of many Asian leaders also affects business, which prefers a stable and predictable political environment and policy framework. Finally and very importantly, there is mounting evidence that the U.S. economic boom has finally run its course. The United States remains the most important single market for many Asian economies, most notably China and Malaysia.

MISSILE SYSTEMS   Turning from the short to the long term, the 2001 *Outlook* team identified the interconnected issues of tensions across the Taiwan Strait, uncertainties in Sino-U.S. relations, and rapid Chinese military modernization as by far the most significant threats to regional security. Most of the analysts see the development of missile defense systems by the United States (in cooperation with Japan and possibly others) as a potentially seriously destabilizing element in the picture.

The key dynamic is that Chinese leaders find even a modest national missile defense (NMD) system and theater missile defense (TMD) system threatening to their very limited strategic deterrent. Most of the *Outlook* team regarded the Clinton administration's postponement of the decision on deploying an NMD as positive. However, this delayed rather than resolved the issue. The assessments of the United States and Japan contained in this report indicate that, despite technical and financial problems in developing an effective missile defense system, domestic political considerations in both countries ensure that missile defense development will continue in some form. The *Outlook* analysts see it as essential for regional peace and security that the United States and China handle this set of issues successfully.

WEAK REGIONAL INSTITUTIONS   The perceived danger posed by the above issues is magnified by the weak institutional capacity that is available to deal with them. There have been relatively successful peacekeeping operations in Asia Pacific, such as in Cambodia in the early 1990s and in East Timor at the end of the decade. However, both of these operations required international and UN sponsorship. The *Outlook 2001* analysts overwhelmingly agree on the desirability of strengthening and expanding various multilateral forums as well as subregional dialogues (particularly in Northeast Asia) as a means of enhancing regional confidence and security. However, the capabilities and future of Asia Pacific multilateral institutions, principally the Asia-Pacific Economic Cooperation (APEC) forum and the ASEAN Regional Forum (ARF), seem to be subject to major shortcomings. It appears that the operational effectiveness and potential of these institutions were overestimated, much more so for APEC than for ARF. The 1997–1998 economic crisis and the 1999 East Timor crisis provided a stark demonstration of the limits of APEC and ARF in each situation. APEC continues to flourish as a venue for dialogue among ministers and leaders, but its own economic liberalization efforts have stalled. ARF has been remarkably successful in expanding its membership (North Korea joined this year) and in fostering some confidence-building measures. On the other side of the ledger, its efforts to move into the area of preventive diplomacy have proven difficult, and peacekeeping or conflict prevention activities seem well beyond the realm of the possible for the near future.

THE WATCH LIST

Since its inception in 1997, the *Asia Pacific Security Outlook* has monitored four "watch list" issues: the Korean peninsula, large power relations, arms acquisitions, and territorial disputes. Last year's volume also gave prominence to the situation in Indonesia. These five items are of such importance to fundamental regional stability that they should continue to be carefully monitored.

The *Outlook 2001* team generally saw little change in Korea and on territorial issues. Some loosening in North Korea's external relationships was noted, but this was offset by Pyongyang's continuing economic deterioration and the use of nuclear and missile development as a bargaining tool. The major territorial disputes (especially the issue of maritime claims in the South China Sea) continued to fester but seemed unlikely to trigger serious military conflict in the near term. However, more serious concerns were expressed over trends in large power relations and weapons procurement.

The current assessments of developments in 2000 and the outlook for 2001 see both Korea and (to a lesser degree) major power relations as improved. As suggested above, Indonesia's situation has deteriorated. No significant changes were registered for the other watch list issues.

Although it is accepted that the process on the Korean peninsula is still unpredictable and reversible, many analysts believe that the two Koreas have crossed a major threshold toward previously unimagined possibilities for improved relations and eventual peaceful resolution of the division on the peninsula. There are significant differences between the current rapprochement in inter-Korean relations and earlier episodes. First, this time the heads of state are engaged and committed. This is particularly important in North Korea, where significant change requires the blessing of the leader. Second, improvements in North-South relations are being mirrored in increased dialogue between North Korea and Japan, on one the hand, and North Korea and the United States, on the other. At the beginning of 2001, Washington was even speculating that North Korea might abandon its missile program in return for a visit from the U.S. president. North Korea's entry into the ARF was also seen as a positive step toward engagement in a larger Asia Pacific setting.

That said, North-South progress remains painstakingly slow. Despite Kim Jong Il's interest in economic modernization, his government continues to be concerned about the political repercussions of opening too quickly to the South. Family visits have been highly controlled, and the process of working out the details in such areas as connecting rail links and power grids is far more difficult than the general statements of intentions indicate. The danger is that unless there is continued visible progress in North-South relations, patience with the process will wear thin and recriminations over who is to blame for the lack of progress will overwhelm the current positive atmosphere.

While the *Outlook 2001* team remains concerned over the potential for mismanagement of large power relations, the critical U.S.-China relationship appeared to stabilize during 2000. This was illustrated by the careful handling by all parties of the unprecedented election of Chen Shui-bian, a leader of the pro-independence Democratic Progressive Party, as president in Taiwan. The U.S. approval of permanent normal trade relations with China, ending controversial year-by-year renewals, was another important development in Sino-American relations. Nevertheless, the advent of a new U.S. administration and the impending leadership rotation in China serve as reminders that these relationships are exposed to domestic political leadership changes and need to be constantly reinforced.

The change in U.S. leadership could well lead to early tests of intention. The new U.S. administration will be facing an early decision on arms sales to Taiwan, an area where Beijing will want to set down markers. The Bush administration's stated determination to move ahead with missile defense systems and to strengthen the U.S.-Japan alliance also presents Beijing with difficult policy choices. It has vehemently protested such directions in the past. Both the new U.S. administration and the Chinese leadership, however, may be anxious to avoid rhetorical squabbles that have so frequently bedeviled the relations between Beijing and Washington.

The great majority of the *Outlook 2001* team regards the overall outlook for peaceful resolution of territorial disputes in Asia Pacific as unchanged from previous years. However, although it was not specifically addressed in the original *Outlook* watch list, another source of concern and controversy in 1999—humanitarian intervention in internal conflicts—appeared to diminish in urgency during 2000. Due to the recent experiences in Kosovo and East Timor, this issue was a regular theme in discussions of regional (and international) security throughout 2000. However, by year-end it seemed clear that these two cases reflected individual, unique circumstances and did not establish a precedent for frequent interventions elsewhere.

This leaves questions of weapons development, procurement, and deployment as the major watch list concerns for 2001. Military modernization programs and increases in defense spending and procurement by major regional states (e.g., China and India as well as Japan), show no signs of slackening and could lead to a destabilizing cycle of responses. (An overview of current levels of defense spending and armed forces in the region is provided in table 1.) The most immediate concerns center on the dual issues of missile defense and the proliferation of weapons of mass destruction (including but not limited to nuclear weapons) and associated delivery technologies. The possible impact of missile defense on U.S.-China relations and security in Northeast Asia has been noted. Although 2000 saw no significant nuclear weapons developments in either South Asia or North Korea, continued tensions between India and Pakistan over Jammu and Kashmir and the continuing unpredictability of North Korean actions give these areas high uncertainty and potential volatility.

Table 1. Asia Pacific Defense Spending and Armed Forces (1999)

Country	Defense Spending[a]			GDP		Armed Forces[b]				Population	
	US$ m.	% GDP	Rank	US$ m.	Rank	Number	Rank	% Pop.	Rank	in 1,000s	Rank
United States	275,500	3.0	7	9,200,000	1	1,365,800	3	.50	8	275,636	4
Europe (EU/NATO)[c]	158,438	2.1	12	7,526,300	2	1,588,949	2	.45	10	354,203	3
Japan	40,800	0.9	21	4,300,000	3	236,700	11	.19	17	126,840	7
China[d]	39,500	5.4	3	732,000	5	2,470,000	1	.20	15	1,255,000	1
Russia	31,000	2.8	10	1,100,000	4	1,004,100	6	.69	6	146,000	6
India	14,200	3.2	6	440,000	7	1,303,000	4	.13	20	1,016,242	2
South Korea	12,000	2.9	9	407,000	8	683,000	7	1.44	4	47,500	11
Canada	7,800	1.2	19	644,000	6	59,100	16	.20	16	29,512	12
Australia	7,800	2.0	13	399,000	9	50,600	17	.26	13	19,292	15
Singapore	4,700	3.3	5	144,000	10	60,500	15	1.46	3	4,130	18
Thailand	2,600	1.9	15	135,000	12	301,000	9	.48	9	62,400	10
North Korea	2,100	14.3	1	14,700	17	1,082,000	5	5.03	1	21,500	14
Malaysia	1,800	2.3	11	78,000	14	96,000	14	.44	11	21,868	13
Philippines	1,600	2.0	14	78,500	13	106,000	13	.14	18	77,268	9
Indonesia	1,500	1.1	20	140,000	11	297,000	10	.14	19	206,213	5
Vietnam	890	3.0	8	30,000	16	484,000	8	.59	7	82,014	8
New Zealand	824	1.6	17	51,000	15	9,230	18	.24	14	3,860	19
Brunei	402	6.7	2	6,000	18	5,000	20	1.51	2	332	21
Cambodia	176	5.0	4	3,500	19	140,000	12	1.29	5	10,879	16
Papua New Guinea	46	1.4	18	3,200	20	4,400	21	.09	21	4,862	17
Mongolia	19	1.9	16	980	21	9,100	19	.37	12	2,460	20

SOURCE: Based on data from The Military Balance 2000/2001. London: International Institute for Strategic Studies (IISS), 2000.

[a]Defense spending figures are IISS estimates of total defense spending (not official budgets).

[b]Figures are for active duty regular armed forces.

[c]Europe figures are for the 12 members of the European Union that are also members of the North Atlantic Treaty Organization: Belgium, Denmark, France, Germany, Greece, Italy, Luxembourg, the Netherlands, Norway, Portugal, Spain, and the United Kingdom.

[d]GDP and defense spending estimates for China are based on purchasing power parity, including extra-budgetary military spending (China's official 1999 defense budget was US$12.6 billion).

TOWARD A MORE "NORMAL" REGIONAL COMMUNITY

With the exceptions previously noted, the attention of regional governments and societies tends to be devoted to individual, largely domestic concerns. China almost uniformly insists that it wants to give priority to domestic economic reforms and restructuring and would like to avoid external problems. The Philippines is similarly anxious to avoid external conflicts (e.g., with China in the South China Sea) while it deals with regional insurgencies. The two Koreas are overwhelmingly focused on their respective futures and relationship. Japan remains concerned over its weak economy and government. Indonesia is grappling with fundamental problems of internal stability. Australia is reviewing its security policies and defense spending. And in the United States, the new administration will have to reassess American interests and priorities in the region, in the context of global commitments, and attempt to develop or at least restate or modify basic policies.

Thus, the Asia Pacific environment in 2001 makes for a far more diverse set of issues across the region, and also appears to be supporting a general desire to dampen international tensions. One immediate result is an increased interest in dialogue, as governments compare notes and attempt to reduce dangers of external confrontation that could jeopardize domestic agendas. Many of these dialogues are quite superficial and consciously avoid the most vexing issues. Nonetheless, the very process of interchange seems to be making Asia Pacific more of a regional community. Despite instances of serious tensions and the acknowledged weaknesses of the region's formal institutions and other arrangements for mediating problems, underlying trends may offer long-term promise.

ASIA PACIFIC SECURITY OUTLOOK 2001

1 Australia

The Security Environment

During the year 2000, the East Timor crisis, the persistence of Indonesia's problems, the protracted instability in Fiji, and the onset of ethnic conflict in the Solomon Islands reinforced the impression that Australia is situated in an area of instability. While causes of instability vary from case to case, there is a general impression that Australia's security has diminished and that Australia needs to devote more attention to its immediate surroundings.

To Australia, Indonesia is by far the most important of its northern neighbors. Relations with Jakarta were seriously damaged during the East Timor crisis. The Australian government so far has not been able to address adequately the possible effects of Indonesia's diminishing capacity to contribute to regional leadership or to grasp the historic opportunities provided by Indonesia's evolving democracy.

The combined result of the Asian financial crisis and the turmoil in East Timor has led to a notable reduction in Australia's enthusiasm for regional engagement. The Association of Southeast Asian Nations (ASEAN) itself and individual member countries, as neighbors, are still accorded priority, but there is a sense of uncertainty about the potential and direction of regional cooperation in the short and medium term.

In Australia's view, major power relations in the region, especially among China, India, Japan, and the United States, will have the most bearing on the future of the region. Above all, Australia sees the United States as essential to holding in check any potential for strategic competition between major powers in the region.

Discussions in Australia on the major areas of tension in Northeast Asia tend to reflect Australia's sense of being a marginal rather than a principal actor. Australia recognizes that it can only be a minor contributor to the resolution of issues such as the future of Taiwan or stability on the Korean peninsula. The country's main contribution is likely to be made through its political support of the efforts of larger powers or multilateral institutions. Australia has supported the relaxation of tensions on the Korean peninsula in 2000 and reestablished bilateral relations with Pyongyang. Australia also supports the developing interest in some more formalized grouping of those with major stakes in Northeast Asian security.

Concerns about Australia's increased insecurity in Asia Pacific prodded the government to undertake a major public consultation exercise during 2000. Prime Minister John Howard personally launched a public discussion paper in June, and teams held meetings across the country to seek community input for the review process.

The discussion paper laid out broad perspectives for public consideration. It noted that, although Australia is a secure country, it is located in an "extraordinarily dynamic, complex and unpredictable region." Specifically, the discussion paper mentioned two points. First, positive economic growth in most of Asia is likely to increase the defense capabilities of a number of countries. These capabilities can be expected to create new security challenges, since the emergence of new strategic powers always "poses challenges in accommodating their legitimate expectations for increased influence," raising "a longer-term question about Australia's strategic weight in the region." As a result of this situation, the discussion paper concluded that basing long-term defense planning on specific predictions about the strategic future of Asia is quite futile. Second, the paper asserted that Australia's nearby regions, chiefly maritime Southeast Asia and the nearer South Pacific, are experiencing "distinct changes." Separatist pressures and sectarian issues in Indonesia were noted, as was the weakening of social cohesion in Papua New Guinea (PNG) and the Solomon Islands.

The public consultation exercise indicated general support for some increase in defense spending, although the scale of the increase was not specified. It became clear that the public wanted the increase to be applied to the defense of Australia rather than, for example, peacekeeping.

Defense Policies and Issues

THE DEFENSE POLICY WHITE PAPER   In reviewing Australia's defenses, the government needed first to address the troubles facing its defense establishment. These troubles include the budgetary crisis resulting from the over-commitment of limited resources and the deficiencies revealed by the experience of fielding a force in East Timor, particularly the deficiencies in ground forces. However, the government went beyond addressing these issues and late in 2000 produced a white paper outlining capability developments for the next ten years.

The white paper states that Australia faces four distinct defense priorities: first, the defense of Australia and its direct approaches; second, "to foster the security of Australia's immediate neighborhood"; third, to work with other powers to promote stability and cooperation in Southeast Asia; and fourth, "to contribute in appropriate ways to maintaining strategic stability in the wider Asia Pacific region." These priorities are seen as being pursued in close cooperation with allies, neighbors, and regional partners. Australia's alliance with the United States is clearly reaffirmed, including Australia's reliance on extended deterrence against the remote possibility of a nuclear attack. Similarly, Australia's interest in working with the Indonesian government "to establish over time a new defense relationship" is restated, while New Zealand continues to be regarded as a "valued defense partner." Finally, Australia sees itself as the primary supporter of PNG's defense and remains committed to being "the key strategic partner" in the Southwest Pacific.

The white paper also outlines a military strategy in support of Australia's defense priorities, with greatest importance given to the defense of Australia. Australia's defense basically involves the capacity of its forces to defend the country's shores without relying on the combat forces of other countries. Australia must therefore be able to control its air and sea approaches, and, although the country's general military posture should be defensive, Australian forces should be prepared to attack hostile forces as far from the coast as possible. Australia's military strategy also seeks to contribute to the security of Australia's nearest neighbors, not only in time of war but also in responding to nonmilitary needs such as peacekeeping and natural disasters. Finally, defense forces should support Australia's wider interests by contributing to international activities intended to resolve crises beyond Australia's immediate neighborhood.

The white paper identifies a need for increased defense funding over the next ten years. The funding is "front-end loaded" in order to meet the immediate crisis in the defense budget and to provide solutions to the problems revealed by the East Timor experience. In the fiscal year 2000–2001 budget, A$450 million (US$252 million at A$1 = US$0.56) has been provided for East Timor, and this will form part of the funding base for the future defense program. To this will be added A$500 million (US$280 million) in fiscal 2001–2002 and A$1,000 million (US$560 million) in the following financial year, with defense spending to be increased by 3 percent in real terms each year thereafter until fiscal 2010–2011.

These long-term commitments have aroused some skepticism, however. Even if successive governments hold to the commitments, defense spending at the end of the ten-year period would still be only around a relatively modest 1.9 percent of Australia's gross domestic product. While this would bring a halt to the continuing decline in the proportion of GDP for defense, difficulties in meeting recruiting targets suggest that pressures for ongoing increases in personnel costs are likely to grow.

Some support for the commitments' durability can be found in the substantive capability plan contained in the white paper. This plan seeks to provide clear, long-term goals—with costs—for the development of capabilities. Although cost estimates projected as far as ten years into the future can only be regarded as indicative, they can lead to realistic and practical decisions. For example, the substantive capability plan has eschewed notions of developing ground forces capable of fighting in high-intensity battlefields such as Korea, or deploying blue-water naval power based on some form of aircraft carrier group. Instead, priority has been given to remedying the deficiencies revealed by the Australian experience in East Timor, and in the longer term dealing with problems of bloc obsolescence. It is in respect to this latter area that the white paper offers clear, realistic decisions:

(1) Replace the F/A 18 fighters and F-111 bombers from about 2006, but leave open the options of a greater emphasis on missiles and of using a single type of aircraft where currently two are used;

(2) Acquire Airbourne Early Warning aircraft—four in the short term and possibly three more later;

(3) Undertake major refurbishment or replacement of P3C maritime patrol aircraft;

(4) Replace the combat systems and make all other modifications

needed to bring the six Collins-class submarines to full potential;

(5) Equip the navy eventually with three air warfare–capable destroyers that will start entering service only after the ten-year span of the white paper;

(6) Increase the army slightly in size, with six battalion groups to be kept at high readiness;

(7) Acquire two squadrons of armed reconnaissance helicopters and another squadron of troop-lift helicopters; and

(8) Round out ground force capability by changing the role of the Reserves, upgrading armored personnel carriers, and acquiring thermal imaging, body armor, air defense mortars, and anti-armor weapons.

The white paper shows that there has been a substantial change in thinking from earlier attempts to revive "forward defense." The capability plans outlined in the paper match Australia's strategic priorities coherently, especially concerning the defense of Australia. This change has been rewarded with a restoration of bipartisan support. But the manpower of the full-time force will be kept to a modest 54,000 even at the end of the ten-year period.

A stronger focus on Australia's neighborhood has also brought an acknowledgment of the nonmilitary pressures facing the country's security. These include illegal immigration, drug trafficking, illegal fishing, quarantine infringements, and terrorism. As a result, the Australian Defense Force (ADF) has introduced measures to promote closer coordination with the civil coastal surveillance system and continues to contribute to coastal surveillance. The government, however, has again declined to establish a coast guard, as the opposition proposed.

An issue that has arisen in reaction to the white paper is how the causes of instability in the region can be addressed by other than military means, and how various policy areas can be coordinated to support nonmilitary solutions. By their nature, problems in developing neighbor countries are likely to require assistance and support for improved governance. Some commentators have questioned whether current levels of effort are adequate in these areas. Australia's aid effort, which is concentrated in its own neighborhood, has been falling in proportion to GDP. Official Development Assistance (ODA) in 2000–2001 will be only 0.25 percent of GDP.

THE DEFENSE BUDGET   Pressures on the defense budget grew during 1999 and 2000. The East Timor commitment stretched resources to the point where a special tax was introduced (though it was lifted in 2000) and an ad hoc addition made to the already approved defense budget. The effect of the East Timor commitment can be seen in the allocation to defense of A$740 million (US$414.4 million) in fiscal 1999–2000 to cover additional costs. Thus, after taking account of additional funding provided in 1999–2000, the share of GDP allocated to defense in fiscal 2000–2001 of 1.8 percent represents a decline from 1.9 percent in the preceding year.

Total defense funding in fiscal 2000–2001 increased in nominal terms by A$651 million (US$364.56 million) to A$18.62 billion (US$10.42 billion) on an accrual basis. In real terms, however, there has been zero growth. Defense budgeting includes a "capital use charge" assessed at 12 percent per year. If this is deducted, it is possible to identify total appropriations, which are A$12.2 billion (US$6.83 billion) in fiscal 2000–2001 and projected to rise to $A12.74 billion (US$7.13 billion) in fiscal 2003–2004, thus maintaining zero real growth. A reflection of the tight funding for defense in fiscal 2000–2001 is that no new funding for facilities projects was approved. Only A$124.2 million (US$69.55 million) was provided for ongoing projects, of which the most significant is the upgrading of barracks and facilities at Townsville, Nowra, and Darwin.

Total funding for equipment projects in fiscal 2000–2001 is A$3.33 billion (US$1.86 billion). New large-scale projects were held back in anticipation of the white paper. Ongoing projects that continue to receive funding are listed in table 1.

Specific priorities included in the budget relate to the following areas:

Table 1. Ongoing Military Projects Receiving Funding in Australia

Maritime and Ground Forces	Aerospace	Electronic Systems
Anzac frigate construction	Lead-in fighter (Hawk)	Military satellite communications
Frigate upgrade	P3C update	
Minehunter coastal acquisition	Anzac ship surveillance helicopters	Over-the-horizon radar
New submarine (Collins-class)	Air-to-air weapons for F/A 18 fighters	High-frequency communications modernization
Seasparrow missile	Air-to-surface standoff weapons	Tactical air defense
Infantry mobility vehicles	F/A 18 fighter upgrade	Defense air traffic control system
Armored personnel carrier upgrade	Strategic airlift (C130J)	
	Seahawk helicopter electronics development	

"fixing problem equipment projects," principally the Collins-class submarines; preparing for decisions on major equipment platforms; adopting a whole-of-capability/whole-of-life perspective in developing ADF capabilities; ensuring that the reserves can be used effectively; addressing the sustainability of combat capability; and continuing measures to "restore confidence" in the defense organization through organizational renewal.

CONTRIBUTION TO REGIONAL AND GLOBAL SECURITY

Australia provides an ongoing deployment of approximately 1,500 personnel to the UN Transitional Administration in East Timor (UNTAET). The Australian force serves mainly on the sensitive border with Indonesia. In response to a request from East Timor's leaders, Australia has committed itself to this level of effort beyond the term of UNTAET. The government has said that the East Timor contribution may last "some time," but has not attempted to specify an end point. The budget for fiscal 2000–2001 provides A$949 million (US$531.44 million) for UN operations in East Timor, gradually decreasing to A$699 million (US$391.44 million) in fiscal 2003–2004. In addition, Australia will provide aid—A$150 million (US$84 million) over four years—for the reconstruction and development of East Timor.

During 2000, Australia's involvement with the security of Papua New Guinea started to grow again as a result of Papua New Guinea's deteriorating Defense Force. The PNG Defense Force has suffered over the last decade under the strain of Bougainville's separatist activities. This resulted in deterioration to the point where the Defense Force's inability to conduct military operations was seen as posing a threat to public order.

While previous differences between Canberra and Port Moresby came to a head as Papua New Guinea attempted to engage foreign mercenaries in the Bougainville conflict, the country's reformist government recently appealed for Australian aid. Australia is now committed to providing up to 30 personnel to assist Defense Force reform with the objective of lowering the number of PNG forces drastically from 4,200 to 1,500 by mid-2000. This reform assistance will also require A$5 million (US$2.8 million) in a one-time package to cover the financial commitments incurred by the PNG Defense Force. In its entirety, Australia's defense assistance to Papua New Guinea will mark a threefold rise to a total of some A$25 million (US$14 million) in fiscal 2000–2001. In addition, Australia continues to provide support for the peace process in Bougainville: 245 personnel out of a total of 306 supporting the Bougainville process come from Australia.

Finally, ethnic conflict between two island communities in the Solomon Islands has produced a continuing Australian involvement. At first Australia was slow to recognize the significance of growing violence. Initial responses were low-key and perceived as ineffective. The Australian government preferred to facilitate a negotiated solution to the conflict, although public pressure and requests from the Solomon Islands called for some form of direct military or police role.

The government's patience was rewarded in October 2000 as peace talks in Townsville produced an agreement on the cessation of hostilities, surrender of arms, and repatriation of personnel. In an arrangement that builds on the model of the Bougainville peace process, both sides agreed that surrendered weapons would remain for two years on the home islands of the previously conflicting sides. Arms would also be kept under the supervision of an unarmed, international, peace-monitoring group. The size and composition of the group is expected to be comparable to the one in Bougainville and will thus require some 200 Australian personnel. In addition, the Solomons agreement provides for accelerated economic development and improved health and education services on the two island provinces primarily concerned. Consequently, the agreement specifies that there should be self-government for all nine of Solomons' provinces. This will place an increased strain on already stretched political and administrative resources, requiring substantial civil aid from the international community, with Australia expected to provide the bulk of the aid.

2 Brunei Darussalam

During 2000, no specific security concerns faced Brunei Darussalam, and the country enjoyed a period of internal peace and stability. Like other states, Brunei experienced a nervous transition into the final year of the 20th century, fearful of the much-hyped "millennium bug." Despite the global scare, the sultanate's highest civilian official in the Ministry of Defense (who is also the chairman of the state's national airlines) flew on a special millennium flight to Australia. This provided a positive image for the future of this tradition-bound yet modernizing society and underlined changes in perceptions of information and communication technology that had been stressed throughout the year.

Known for its political stability and low levels of crime, Brunei's attitude toward security has been almost complacent. The country's outlook changed somewhat as the sultanate chaired the Asia-Pacific Economic Cooperation (APEC) forum in 2000 and hosted the APEC summit. The APEC year produced a hard look at how to assure a peaceful and secure environment. This emphasis was reinforced by the fact that 2001 has been designated "Visit Brunei Year" and, toward the end of the year, Brunei will host the Association of Southeast Asian Nations (ASEAN) leaders' summit. The APEC summit meeting proved a success. Observers speculated on whether, after exposure to at least a thousand media personnel covering the APEC events, Brunei might evolve toward a more open system.

Despite diversification efforts, Brunei's economy remains heavily dependent on oil and gas revenues. During the Asian economic crisis, Brunei experienced a slowdown. This was mainly due to lower oil prices, which led to a loss of revenue and influenced spending by the government—the largest single player in the economy. To counter the slowdown, the Brunei Darussalam Economic Development Council (which had released a report and recommendations in September 1999) implemented a number of short-term measures to boost economic growth. In particular, assistance to local small and medium-sized enterprises was extended to tackle the country's 6 percent unemployment rate by creating jobs for the young, who are most likely to be unemployed. In addition, oil, gas, and investment revenues are continuing to contribute to national expenditure, with the government committed to sustaining the country's comfortable lifestyle supported by "welfare" spending. Finally, tourism was identified as a possible new source of income. The last couple of years have seen vigorous attempts by government agencies to market Brunei as a tourism destination in its own right, together with the neighboring Borneo states of Sabah and Sarawak, and also to emphasize Brunei's membership in ASEAN.

Following the collapse of the Amedeo Development Corporation during the economic crisis, when the company lost several billion U.S. dollars, Brunei's government tried both to put the company's assets to positive use and to recover some of the losses. Some of the expansive infrastructure built by Amedeo was used to host APEC meetings and visiting delegations in 2000. Its buildings will also be used at the beginning of 2001 for a large meeting and exhibition—the ASEAN Tourism Forum—in Bandar Seri Begawan. Through the Brunei Investment Agency, the government has purchased some of Amedeo's property and is trying to recover lost state funds. Moreover, court proceedings have been initiated against a number of people accused of embezzling state funds, including the sultan's brother and the former minister of finance.

Brunei has not had to worry about regional conflicts affecting its territory. Ethnic conflicts in Indonesia have been widely reported in the local press, but hardly any support is voiced for Islamic separatist movements like those in Aceh or Mindanao. In fact, there is much more concern and support for the Palestinian cause because it involves Islam's holy places. The kidnapping of tourists and Malaysians from islands off Sabah in April and September 2000 and the daily television images of these incidents stirred some local debate. Noticeably, the Abu Sayaf Group (ASG) lost sympathizers after it became apparent that an economic motive, ransom, was the central issue, rather than any Islamic cause.

Piracy has not been an issue on the western coast of Borneo. However, the sultanate has been vigilant in stopping illegal immigrants, who, coming mainly from Mindanao, sneak into the country through Brunei's land and sea borders with Malaysia.

In Brunei Darussalam, regime loyalty and state survival rely on adherence to the national ideology (Melayu Islam Beraja, or Malay Islamic Monarchy), which incorporates a strict national interpretation of Islam. Consequently, the July 2000 incident in the Malaysian state of Perak when the Al Ma'unah (Brotherhood of Inner Power) group stole weapons from an army camp and subsequently clashed with antiterrorist commandos attracted considerable interest, especially as there were a number of Al Ma'unah followers in Brunei. A Brunei branch had been set up in late 1999, but was not registered legally. The Al Ma'unah, which trains in Muslim martial arts, believes in holy war to preserve its interpretation of Islam. In light of the Perak incident, Brunei authorities felt that the group's potential for violence could not be underestimated. Authorities branded the Al Ma'unah's teachings as deviationist, issued a stern warning to the group's followers, and detained a number of (mostly Bruneian) individuals for questioning.

The general consensus was that the group in Brunei had merely been involved in "*silat*," the art of Muslim self-defense, and did not pose a threat to national security. Al Ma'unah shared the fate of another Islamic group originating in Malaysia, the Al-Arquam, which two years earlier also had been banned for unacceptable teachings and practices. In mid-December 2000, the local press reported that an underground Christian group had been identified, and that three local men had been arrested for questioning. Evidently, Bruneian authorities have been wary of religious activities that could destabilize the social and political fabric.

DEFENSE POLICIES AND ISSUES

The mission statement of the Ministry of Defense explains that the professional role of the sultanate's defense force is "to preserve the independence, security, national sovereignty, peace, territorial integrity, and the national interests of Brunei Darussalam." It also states that the ministry provides support services to other government agencies. The sultan, Haji Hassanal Bolkiah, as head of state and government, continues as minister of defense, with a retired major general as his deputy. The ministry's policies and functions show a close link between civilian and military duties, although the armed forces are responsible for defense matters while bureaucrats deal with civilian affairs. Structurally, the defense forces are divided into the land force, navy, air force, and services force, with other units engaged in training and intelligence tasks. Each May, on Armed Forces Day, the military is recognized for its contributions. Unlike in some states, however, in Brunei there are no mass displays of military personnel or weaponry.

The military's domestic role was of special significance in 2000. During the APEC summit, the largest international event ever held in Brunei, the armed forces' role was expanded to include providing security and safety to visitors and residents. Together with the police force, the military participated in planning and exercising all aspects of security and logistics, with government spending reaching US$35 million for APEC logistics alone. To date, this is the largest joint operation undertaken by the military and police forces.

Brunei's small defense and security establishment greatly facilitated close coordination during the APEC summit. Several mock attacks, demonstrations, bomb threats, and drills were conducted to test the preparedness of all units. Evidently, the sometimes violent demonstrations that had occurred during recent international trade meetings in Seattle, Washington, D.C., and Melbourne concerned Brunei's security establishment. However, the APEC summit took place without incident. Some attributed the smooth summit to Brunei's relative isolation, while others pointed to the lack of a tradition of mass participation in local politics. Whatever the reasons, this experience will reinforce the cooperative atmosphere among the various services in Brunei's security network.

During 2000, the armed forces undertook no major recruitment drives, with new recruits continuing to number about 200 per year. The total number of Brunei's military personnel is below 5,000, while the police force numbers about 2,000. No major changes have occurred in these totals since 1999, with the only exception being a newly created Forest Police of about 200 men that was added to the Royal Brunei Police Force. The Forest Police was established to avert crime in rural areas, especially the illegal logging of primary forests and the smuggling of contraband items such as liquor in border areas.

After two years of a slump in oil prices, the outlook for Brunei's income in 2000 appears good. Brunei stands to gain an extra US$1 billion as a result of the sharp increase in oil prices, reaching US$35 per barrel. Thus, the armed forces, already one of the highest recipients within the government budget, may see an increase in its allocation. Some large orders for military hardware, suspended during the economic recession, may be renewed in the coming budget. Clearly, there is an interest in procuring more specialized training and hardware.

The Brunei government does not publish a defense white paper or specific budgets for military spending. Only the overall budget of the Ministry of Defense is available. For example, in 1998 the ministry's expenditure reached B$492 million (US$284 million at US$1 = B$1.73), only B$150 million (US$87 million) less than the largest spender, the Ministry of Finance. The police spent B$74 million (US$43 million). The Defense Ministry's spending constituted about 13 percent of total government expenditure. By comparison, the Ministry of Education received 10 percent of the budget. As the government seeks to build up the military sector, this general situation is likely to continue. Actual military procurement, however, involves another set of budget figures. One conservative estimate puts these procurements at US$100 million for 1998.

Over the past years, expansion and professionalization of the armed forces has been emphasized, with the sultan taking a direct interest in the training and welfare of military personnel. A number of foreign military leaders met with the sultan (in his capacity as defense minister) and his deputy. Joint exercises with visiting units, for example with the Singaporean air force and the Indonesian and U.S. navies, have taken place. Defense personnel from Malaysia and the Philippines have also been involved in high-level planning meetings. Besides building bilateral defense links with regional countries and the United States, Brunei continues its close political and defense cooperation with the United Kingdom. Its defense force remains heavily reliant on the United Kingdom, and its personnel training closely linked to British programs. Brunei's defense procurement and the presence of foreign troops in Brunei have not upset neighboring countries and have not been viewed as threats. Thus, current bilateral links are very likely to continue at least for the next several years.

CONTRIBUTIONS TO REGIONAL SECURITY

As a small state, Brunei places a great deal of confidence in the ASEAN process of good neighborliness to safeguard its survival. In Brunei's view, the extended role of ASEAN to involve a larger set of dialogue partners through the ASEAN Regional Forum (ARF) assures a certain measure of transparency and confidence building in the region. ASEAN's establishment of formalized links with China, Japan, and South Korea are especially seen as aiding Brunei's relations with these bigger states.

Brunei has also sought to effectively use track-two diplomatic channels. For example, Brunei has regularly participated in the meetings of the ASEAN Institutes for Strategic and International Studies (ASEAN-ISIS), though so far the sultanate has only sent observers from the ministries of foreign affairs and defense. In mid-2000, Brunei set up its own Institute of Policy and Strategic Studies (IPSS) as a department within the Ministry of Foreign Affairs. This local institution is now a full member of the ASEAN-ISIS. It organized the first ISIS workshop for young ASEAN leaders, indicating a strong interest to host and participate in regional meetings. The IPSS may develop into an active policy research institution and thus generate stronger Bruneian awareness, interest, and participation in regional affairs.

ASEAN has collectively addressed the Spratly Islands dispute, although the regional Code of Conduct between ASEAN and China, the largest claimant, has yet to be finalized. Brunei, as the smallest member, claims the smallest share, the Louisa Reef. This reef is also contested by Malaysia, which has reportedly erected a marker there. Neither an immediate threat nor an easy settlement of this issue is anticipated by Brunei. The Louisa Reef is similar to other outstanding border issues that Brunei has with Malaysia, such as the sultanate's historical claim on the Limbang territory, now part of Malaysia's Sarawak. These border issues are being discussed in regular negotiations with Malaysia at the highest levels of government.

Brunei participates seriously and sincerely as a member in regional and international organizations. The sultanate is committed to the ideals of the United Nations, the Commonwealth, and the Organization of the Islamic Conference (OIC). Originally, Brunei was to have been part of a seven-nation OIC team that visited the Philippines in October 2000. In June 2000, the Islamic Conference of Foreign Ministers held in Kuala Lumpur adopted a recommendation to send a fact-finding mission to study the plight of Muslims in Mindanao. This mission, led by the foreign minister of Indonesia, sought to look into the implementation of the OIC-brokered 1996 peace accord between the Philippine government and the Moro National Liberation Front (MNLF). In addition, the Moro Islamic Liberation Front (MILF), which split from the MNLF in 1978, was keen to meet the OIC mission. The mission comprised representatives from Indonesia, Libya, Pakistan, Saudi Arabia, and Senegal, with Brunei included as an additional member later.

However, just days before the mission's departure, it was announced that Brunei would not be participating in the visit because of logistical problems.

Over the past year, the Brunei-Indonesia-Malaysia-Philippines–East ASEAN Growth Area (BIMP-EAGA), of which Brunei is an active member, has experienced some setbacks. Specifically, local businesspeople feared their trade and investment activities would be affected adversely by the shaky security climate in Mindanao. Thus, Brunei businesses have limited their cross-border EAGA activities to Sabah and Sarawak. Leaders of the EAGA have grown increasingly concerned about the continuing violence in Mindanao. They believe that collective efforts toward economic development may eventually bring a peaceful end to the conflict. However, only the Philippines, by reaching a comprehensive domestic settlement in Mindanao, can ultimately ensure a secure environment for businesses to operate.

Finally, the participation of Gurkhas from the British Garrison stationed in Brunei in the peacekeeping efforts in East Timor in 1999 earned the gratitude of the East Timorese. This was expressed by East Timorese leader Xanana Gusmao when he met with the sultan and other ministers on his official visit to Brunei in late May 2000.

3 Cambodia

THE SECURITY ENVIRONMENT

Cambodia entered 2001 having experienced a long period of peace and stability in the year 2000. This internal order was made possible due to the demise of the Khmer Rouge and the establishment of a stable coalition government. However, Cambodia has continued to face challenges, such as the most severe flooding in 40 years, economic stagnation, and controversy over the upcoming trial of the Khmer Rouge.

Several other issues occupied the country in 2000. Cambodia continued efforts begun in 1999 to restructure its armed forces by pursuing a policy of downsizing without reducing defense capabilities. Cambodia also actively developed bilateral and multilateral relations. It will take some time, however, for Cambodia to fully "normalize" relations with all countries and to become more active at the regional and global level.

INTERNAL   In 2000, Cambodia enjoyed greater internal order than in the period before November 1998. However, this order was disrupted on the night of November 24, 2000, when a group of 50 armed men, calling themselves the Cambodian Freedom Fighters, threw grenades and attacked the offices of the Council of Ministers and the Ministry of National Defense and a gasoline station. The attack, which was the worst violence since the fighting in July 1997, resulted in several deaths and a few dozen injuries. It also raised concerns as to whether the period of peace and stability in Cambodia would continue.

Future political stability is questioned in part because of the politically sensitive trial of Khmer Rouge leaders. These trials are demanded by the United Nations and the international community because of past Khmer Rouge crimes against humanity. The coalition parties in the Cambodian government, however, are divided on the issue. To the end of the Khmer Rouge threat, the government pursued a policy of both confrontation and reconciliation, and some agreements made then may be threatened by the trials. Moreover, some Cambodians resent outside involvement in their internal affairs. At the end of 2000, the National Assembly was debating a draft law on conducting the trials with particular attention to a procedure acceptable to the United Nations and to domestic Cambodian interests.

In domestic politics, a reshuffle of the coalition government between the Cambodian People's Party (CPP) and the royalist FUNCINPEC may take place before the end of the first quarter of 2001. Chea Sim, president of the CPP and the Senate, had a stroke in late October 2000. If Chea's health deteriorates, this could have a political impact on the CPP and the coalition government. In 2000, the Sam Rainsy Party (SRP), the only opposition party in Cambodia, also became more vocal and politically active. SRP leader Sam Rainsy and party members confronted the government on a number of issues, ranging from the construction of a memorial stupa to honor Cambodians who died in the March 1997 grenade attack to alleged corruption in the distribution of aid to flood victims. These challenges helped build a culture of political dialogue and increasing political tolerance of the opposition by the ruling government. Whether this trend in Cambodian politics will continue, however, remains to be seen.

Communal elections intended to accelerate democratization and decentralization, originally scheduled for 2000, have not yet taken place. Despite progress on a draft law, the legal framework remains insufficient. Likewise, budget constraints and political differences have hampered progress, although an announcement by the German government that it would contribute US$2 million to organize the elections provided an important impetus. If there is sufficient political will on the part of Cambodia's leaders, the elections may take place in 2001.

The final major issue in Cambodia's domestic politics during 2000 was the royal succession. The health of King Norodom Sihanouk is deteriorating, and the Chinese government reportedly has for the first time suggested that the Cambodian government plan for a succession. Although there is a formal legal procedure in which the Throne Council constitutionally chooses the next king, royal succession is likely to be politically complicated due to the existence of several potential candidates. These include Her Majesty Queen Norodom Sihanouk Monineath, National Assembly President Prince Norodom Ranariddh, Cambodia's Ambassador to UNESCO in Paris Prince Norodom Sihamoni, and the half brother of the current king, Prince Norodom Sirivudh. Certainly the monarchy as an institution will survive in the post-Sihanouk era due to the high regard afforded it by the Cambodian public. However, given King Sihanouk's great personal popularity with Cambodians, questions remain as to how strong the monarchy will be after Sihanouk's departure from the scene.

The most notable nonpolitical event in 2000 was the severe flooding that Cambodia suffered for the first time in 40 years. With the exception of just a few provinces, the floods affected the entire country. More than 200 lives were lost, most crops were destroyed, and major infrastructure, such as roads, bridges, schools, and temples, was damaged. While the total cost of the damage is still not known, estimates are around US$100 million. The Cambodian government diverted part of the national budget to assist flood-affected Cambodians, and the country received millions of dollars in donations for the flood victims.

Before receiving flood donations, the Cambodian government was able to secure pledges of financial assistance in the amount of US$540 million for 2000–2001 at the Consultative Group meeting in Paris on May 24–26, 2000. This exceeded the expectations of the Hun Sen government. It appears that the government's progress in areas such as forestry reform and political stability has convinced the donor community. Indeed, over the past few years, due to the introduction and implementation of new policies and laws, the government has successfully reduced environmental degradation and the exploitation of natural resources.

Despite the donor community's promises of financial aid, however, the Cambodian economy appears to have slowed down for the first time since 1994. Approximately 5 percent economic growth was estimated for 2000, and Cambodia received only US$213 million in pledged investment capital in the first nine months of 2000, the lowest since 1994. Rising oil prices and floods also affected the economy. Finally, Cambodia remains highly dependent on garment and textile exports, a sector that might be affected by developments in U.S.-Vietnam trade relations.

EXTERNAL   *Relations with Great Powers.* While China noted its disapproval of a visit by Sam Rainsy to Taiwan in mid-2000, Cambodia's relations with China remain close. On November 13–15, Chinese

President Jiang Zemin became the first Chinese head of state to visit Cambodia since 1963. At the request of Cambodia, China also provided US$100 million in loans to Cambodia for the development of agriculture and irrigation works. In addition, investment flows and tourist arrivals from China have increased substantially.

Relations between Cambodia and the United States during 2000 were complicated by differences over the Khmer Rouge trial. The United States would like to see the trial of former Khmer Rouge leaders move forward rapidly. However, as noted earlier, the trial may not take place due to its political and security implications for the Cambodian government. Despite these differences, in 2000 the United States extended tariff preferences to Cambodia and lifted limitations on the issuance of U.S. visas to Cambodians.

On January 10–12, 2000, the late Japanese Prime Minister Obuchi Keizō paid an official visit to Cambodia, marking the first time a Japanese prime minister had visited Cambodia in 43 years. During his visit, Obuchi pledged to provide grant aid of ¥849 million (US$7.39 million at US$1 = ¥114.75). Japan thus has remained Cambodia's number one donor since 1994.

Relations with Neighboring Countries. Cambodia's relations with Thailand improved in several areas during 2000. In late January, Cambodia and Thailand held the Third Meeting of the Joint Commission for Bilateral Cooperation led by their respective foreign ministers. During an official visit by Prime Minister Chuan Leekpai to Cambodia in June, several important agreements were signed, including an agreement on combating illicit cross-border smuggling of cultural properties, another on repatriating stolen vehicles, and a memorandum of understanding on surveying and demarcating land boundaries. Several alleged border encroachments by the Thai military took place during the first six months of 2000, however, lending greater urgency to the second meeting of the Cambodian-Thai Joint Commission on Demarcating the Land Boundary held on June 5–7, 2000.

Cambodia-Vietnam relations faced many challenges in 2000, including disputes over immigration, trade, and land and maritime borders. In September, Cambodian border chief Var Kim Hong led a delegation by helicopter to examine the Cambodian border with Vietnam. Although the Cambodian side had informed its Vietnamese counterparts about this flight, the helicopter was refused landing and was almost shot down by Vietnamese border patrols.

Despite this incident, high-level diplomatic exchanges continued between the two countries. Both Vietnam's Foreign Minister Nguyen Dy Nien and Deputy Prime Minister Nguyen Tan Dung visited Cambodia on separate occasions; Cambodia's Co-Defense Minister Prince Sisowath Sirirath led a delegation to Vietnam; and in early October, the Communist Party of Vietnam reestablished relations with FUNCINPEC when the second vice-president of Cambodia's Senate, Nhiek Bun Chhay, visited Hanoi. However, a scheduled visit by Vietnamese President Tran Duc Luong to Cambodia on November 27–28 was canceled due to the attack in Phnom Penh by the Cambodian Freedom Fighters on November 24. During the year, Cambodia and Vietnam signed three agreements: on scientific and technical cooperation in agriculture, forestry, and fisheries; on accounting; and on the repatriation of the remains of Vietnamese volunteer soldiers killed in action. A memorandum of understanding on cooperation in health care was also signed.

DEFENSE POLICIES AND ISSUES

DEFENSE POLICY   According to reports on the Ministry of National Defense's white paper now in preparation, Cambodia faces no immediate military threat. This assessment is based on three factors: (1) sucessful national reconciliation that has brought greater peace and stability to Cambodia; (2) strict adherence to the policy of "amity" with regional countries; and (3) a strong commitment to confidence-building measures. Cambodia's defense policy emphasizes the following objectives:
- Maintain sufficient capacity to ensure stability and order;
- Protect the nation's borders;
- Reshape the Royal Cambodian Armed Forces (RCAF) into a smaller, more professional military force;
- Contribute to national development;
- Develop enhanced capacity to protect the country's maritime areas; and
- Engage in confidence-building measures with neighboring countries.

To fulfill these objectives, the RCAF's functions have been defined as follows:
- Direction of the nation's defense and its strategic interests;
- Promotion of national development;
- Cooperation with the Ministry of Interior in the maintenance of peace, stability, and social order; and
- Participation in international security cooperation.

The RCAF has also been assigned specific functions for promoting national development, such as providing engineering support in the areas of mine clearance, medical assistance, protection of natural resources, and relief operations. However, it is still unclear how the RCAF's involvement in domestic security matters will work out since electoral laws strictly prohibit the RCAF from participating in domestic politics.

DEFENSE BUDGET   Cambodia does not make its defense budget public. Based on informed sources, Cambodia's 2000 defense budget, combined with appropriations for the police under the category "defense and security," was approximately the equivalent of US$119 million, or about 37 percent of the national budget. The budget for defense alone was estimated at US$89 million, a decrease of 4 percent compared to 1999; further cutbacks are expected for 2001. The Cambodian government has come under strong pressure from aid donors to significantly reduce defense and security expenditures and to devote the savings to health and education. However, Cambodia faces tough challenges in reducing its defense and security budget since most of this budget is spent on salaries and other basic military needs, such as rice rations, uniforms, and fuel.

DEMOBILIZATION   The Cambodian government plans to demobilize 55,000 soldiers by 2003. Most of these forces are stationed at the provincial level. At the beginning of 2000, the government began a pilot program of downsizing in Kampot, Kompong Thom, and Kompong Speu provinces. Under this plan, the government pays US$230 to each demobilized soldier. While it is too early to assess the real impact of demobilization, there are reports of security problems in areas where soldiers were demobilized. Clearly, how to reintegrate these soldiers into civilian life is one of the most challenging issues facing the Cambodian government today, with wide-ranging political, economic, and social implications. However, given current civilian control of the military, especially under Prime Minister Hun Sen, it is considered unlikely that demobilization will cause substantial security problems.

FORCE STRUCTURE   Cambodia's security forces number approximately 140,000 for the military and 65,000 for the police. Compiled according to various unofficial sources, table 1 shows past and planned changes in Cambodia's security forces.

Table 1: Personnel Strength of Cambodia's Security Forces

	1997	1998	1999	2000	2001
Police	67,800	65,700	65,000	65,000	65,000
Military	123,100	143,300	140,000	140,000	135,000

DEFENSE COOPERATION   As in recent years, only a few countries actively engaged in defense cooperation with Cambodia during 2000. Australia supported the training of military officials and is assisting in the preparation of a defense white paper. China provided military assistance to Cambodia worth several million U.S. dollars. The United States, however, continued the suspension of its defense cooperation with the Cambodian government.

CONTRIBUTIONS TO REGIONAL AND GLOBAL SECURITY

Despite its preoccupation with internal security, Cambodia made several modest contributions to regional and global peace in 2000. First, since becoming a full member in the Association of Southeast Asian Nations (ASEAN) in 1999 and in the ASEAN Regional Forum (ARF) in 1995, Cambodia has played an active role in these regional institutions. Specifically, it considers the ARF as a key pillar for security in the region. In 2000, Cambodia also sought to enter the Asia-Europe Meeting (ASEM). In October, Foreign Minister Hor Namhong wrote letters to the foreign ministers of ASEAN members; China; South Korea, the ASEM host for 2000; and France, chair of the European Union, requesting their support for Cambodia's entry into ASEM. Cambodia did not receive an official response from ASEM during 2000, but it remains hopeful of joining the group in 2001.

Second, Cambodia, Japan, and Canada agreed to organize the ARF Confidence-Building Measures Seminar in Phnom Penh scheduled for February 2001. Third, the Cambodian government proposed a trilateral meeting with Cambodia, Laos, and Thailand to promote closer cooperation and dialogue between mainland Southeast Asia and ASEAN. This dialogue complemented the 1999 meeting of Cambodia, Laos, and Vietnam. In addition, Cambodia continued to call for closer cooperation in the Greater Mekong Subregion (GMS), believing that a peaceful and stable Mekong region can strengthen regional security.

Fourth, Cambodia sent peacekeepers and land mine clearance experts to Bosnia and Kosovo. As one of the countries most heavily affected by land mines, Cambodia has a continuing interest in sharing its experienced personnel with countries facing land mine removal problems.

Fifth, due to King Norodom Sihanouk's close relationship with North Korean leaders, ASEAN, during its July 2000 meeting in Bangkok, requested Cambodia's help in nudging North Korea to join the ARF. In this manner, Cambodia was able to make a positive contribution to the ARF, to a constructive dialogue related to the unification of the Korean peninsula, and to regional peace and stability.

Finally, in June 2000 the Cambodian Institute for Cooperation and Peace was admitted as a full member to the Council for Security Cooperation in Asia Pacific (CSCAP). An important Cambodian think tank, this institute will actively participate in track-two security dialogues, thus enhancing Cambodia's contribution to the Asia Pacific multilateral security framework.

4 Canada

The Security Environment

Canada may be at a turning point in its perception of the post–cold war security environment. A growing awareness of the dark side of globalization is emerging, diminishing Canada's sense of well-being and social equanimity. In particular, highly publicized incidents of international drug and people trafficking, transnational financial crime, intra-ethnic disputes, and terrorist activities have brought home the realities of the post–cold war world. The election of George W. Bush to the U.S. presidency will also force Canada to face the difficult decision of how to react to U.S. efforts to develop and deploy a national missile defense (NMD) system.

Domestically, the Liberal government of Jean Chrétien was elected to its third term on November 27, 2000. However, Lloyd Axworthy, Canada's foreign minister for four years, left public office. This may produce a reorientation of Canada's foreign policy by the new foreign minister, John Manley, who is likely to emphasize commercial and trade issues. The Canadian government also aired the possibility of a defense policy review in 2001. Major decisions regarding key security matters such as immigration and refugees are on the horizon. Triggered by changes in the global, regional, and domestic arenas, Canada may subtly reorient its foreign and defense policies over the coming years.

GLOBAL SECURITY CONCERNS Canada is deeply and directly affected by the social, economic, and political forces of globalization. Canada's immigration rate compared to its population is the highest in the industrialized world. In 1999, about 80,000 immigrants from Asia alone landed in Canada. Canada is also more closely integrated into the world economy than most countries, deriving 43 percent of its gross domestic product from trade. Since the country's continued prosperity depends on international trade flows, the Canadian government has given strong priority to building an effective rules-based international economic order.

For instance, Canadian Minister of Finance Paul Martin, who in 2000 chaired the Group of 20, has set as one of his priorities the reorganization of international financial institutions. Canadian officials also regard advancement of the World Trade Organization (WTO) as important, even if there has been disappointment over progress to date. The organized opposition that confronted global economic forums in Seattle, Prague, and other places has particularly troubled Canadian policymakers, in part because these policymakers have tried to cultivate a positive attitude toward advancing the role of civil society and non-governmental organizations (NGOs) in international organizations.

Ottawa also regards regional market mechanisms that promote free trade and ensure equal access as vital. However, Canada's experience with the North American Free Trade Agreement (NAFTA) has been double-edged. While Canada's volume of trade has skyrocketed and remains heavily in its favor, friction has remained between Canada and the United States due to what Canadians see as persistent, politically motivated efforts by Washington to engage in unilateral trade restrictions. In addition, Canada remains concerned that existing or proposed trading mechanisms, such as the European Union and the East Asian Economic Caucus, might restrict its market access.

In defense matters, Canadian officials remain particularly concerned about future trends in weapons proliferation, rising threats from terrorism and transnational crime, and heightened ethnic, religious, and national extremism. Major power relations in Canada's view look stable, although Russia and South Asia, especially the volatile India-Pakistan relationship, remain areas of concern.

Over the past five years, Canadian foreign policy has focused on human security. Consequently, Canada has engaged in efforts to engage nonstate actors at national and global levels while it has pushed existing international institutions to be more proactive and promoted nontraditional foreign policy instruments, such as track-two diplomacy, eminent persons groups, and NGO consultations. The Canadian public has generally accepted this new direction in foreign policy. However, Canada's defense and international development establishment has faced difficult challenges in setting priorities and allocating resources across the broad spectrum of human security demands. For instance, it has been difficult for the Department of National Defense (DND) to determine appropriate personnel and equipment allocations, since humanitarian, peace building, and peacekeeping missions all require different capabilities.

Canada's calls for action on human security have met with varying degrees of enthusiasm in international and regional forums. Asian countries, especially China and, to a lesser extent, Japan, have made it clear that their notions of human security encompass much narrower scopes for intervention than do Canada's. The extent to which human security will continue to dominate Canadian foreign and defense policy in the future is uncertain, although the concept of human security will hardly vanish.

REGIONAL SECURITY CONCERNS   For historical, geographic, and social reasons, Canada's primary commitments have been in North America and Europe. Canada has been an enthusiastic participant in the restructuring of the North Atlantic Treaty Organization (NATO), and in recent years the bulk of Canadian military personnel deployed abroad has been in Europe under NATO auspices. Since efforts to develop an independent defense capacity under the European Union exclude Canada by definition, Canadian policymakers remain concerned about their involvement in European regional deliberations.

Although Canada's most extensive institutional ties lie in Europe and North America, Canada's regional security concerns are widely dispersed. In the Americas, membership in the Organization of American States (OAS) has provided Canada with a strong institutional base, allowing it to play a major role in initiatives to promote democratic governance, dispute settlement, and human security. However, in Africa Canadian policymakers remain very reluctant to commit troops to proposed UN missions and are discouraged by the tremendous challenges of the region.

Canada's engagement in Asia Pacific is undergoing subtle changes. While most Asian economies appear to be gradually recuperating from the financial crisis of the late 1990s, Canadian economic engagement with Asia has not recovered to pre–economic crisis levels. The exception is China, where trade with Canada is booming.

Canadian observers regard the Asia Pacific security environment as largely stable. Serious concerns, however, have been raised about Indonesia. Indonesia is seen as fundamental to sustaining regional stability in Southeast Asia, but there is little outside nations can do to help restore order in this country. Canada is also concerned about two other Asian tension points: the Taiwan Strait and South Asia. Here especially, the volatile nature of the Pakistani state and the uncontrollability of the various factions in Jammu and Kashmir may set off a war. On the other hand, improved conditions in Northeast Asia during 2000, especially the inter-Korean summit, are seen as remarkable and positive developments.

From Ottawa's point of view, Asia Pacific regional institutions have lost momentum. The Asia-Pacific Economic Cooperation (APEC) forum appears to have ceded much of its role to the WTO. Its most important role in 2001 and beyond may be to annually convene regional leaders to discuss current crises. On the security side, the ASEAN Regional Forum (ARF) appears unlikely to move beyond its current status as a meeting place, although it remains valuable. This was seen in July 2000 when the North Korean foreign minister attended for the first time.

As a result of these developments in regional institutions, Canada increasingly is emphasizing bilateral relations with Asian countries. Prime Minister Chrétien, often accompanied by Canadian business and political leaders, utilizes high-profile visits to advance commercial interests and to highlight concerns on security and governance matters. In 2000, bilateral engagement with China continued to advance, as seen by the exchange of high-level defense department officials and several activities concerning regional security. Under the "Agenda of Security Cooperation," Canada in partnership with Japan continued to support consultations among officials, academics, and NGOs. Mongolia and Indonesia have also been the focus of considerable Canadian engagement. For example, Indonesia's President Abdurrahman Wahid made a very successful visit to Ottawa in September 2000.

Although a new Liberal majority government and a new foreign minister will determine Canada's foreign policy agenda in 2001, observers anticipate little change in Ottawa's approaches to Asia. Investment and trade relations will remain a top priority, with China, Japan, and Indonesia sustaining their central places on the bilateral agenda. Canada might also modify its policies toward India, which have been static since the nuclear tests of 1998 because of Ottawa's insistence that India join the Nonproliferation Treaty (NPT) as a nonnuclear state.

CONTINENTAL SECURITY   Canada's economic, diplomatic, and military relationship with the United States remains the cornerstone of Canada's national interest and foreign policy. This relationship is institutionalized in a multitude of arrangements including NAFTA and the North American Air Defense (NORAD) agreement. After the accession of the Bush administration, however, certain security-related tensions will likely influence relations in 2001. Primarily these tensions arise from Washington's concern over transnational or asymmetric threats, including industrial and military espionage, the breach of computer networks, illegal trafficking in money, drugs, and people, and terrorism. Elements in the U.S. Congress see Canada as a "weak link" in U.S. efforts to thwart these threats. These concerns were heightened by a highly publicized case in December 1999, when an Algerian national was arrested at the Canada-U.S. border with forged Canadian papers and materials used to make explosives. Subsequent investigations revealed a larger plot to carry out terrorist acts inside the United States as well as the operation of a support network in Canada.

Canada remains concerned that American responses to transnational threats could impede the relatively free flow of goods, services, and people across the Canada-U.S. border. Partially in response to American pressure, the Canadian government committed an extra Can\$1.27 billion (US\$846 million at US\$1 = Can\$1.50) over three years in the 2000 budget to the agencies responsible for security against transnational threats, that is, the Royal Canadian Mounted Police, the Canadian security and intelligence service, Canada Customs, and the Department of Citizenship and Immigration. Recent Canadian defense policy documents have also devoted more attention to how "indirect threats" to national security can be countered by the Canadian military.

In 2001, probably the most important continental security issue facing Canada will be how it should react to the Bush administration's determination to develop and possibly deploy an NMD system. The government of Canada and many voices in the Canadian public have expressed concern that deployment could stimulate an arms race, compromise global nonproliferation regimes such as the Anti-Ballistic Missile (ABM) Treaty, and poison relations with Russia and China. However, a Canadian refusal to participate would have serious implications for NORAD, as well as U.S. perceptions of Canada as a reliable security partner. Therefore, a public and charged airing of NMD and nuclear arms control regime issues can be anticipated for 2001, leaving the government with difficult choices.

DEFENSE POLICIES AND ISSUES

The government of Canada remains officially committed to the 1994 defense white paper. Security policy experts, however, have criticized the paper as being outdated by reinforcing the defense forces' "commitment-capability gap." Between 1993 and 1998, the DND budget fell by 23 percent, with real purchasing power falling by more than 30 percent. As a consequence, Canadian military personnel have been reduced by more than 30 percent (to 60,000) over the last decade, while the Canadian government has mandated larger and more frequent foreign deployments. In 2000, approximately 3,000 Canadian military personnel were deployed abroad in 20 different operations, including almost 1,900 personnel in the Balkans. The result is a military stretched to the limit and afflicted with morale and retention-rate problems.

To counter these problems, the defense budget experienced its second year of growth in 2000. The government also promised to add an additional Can$1.7 billion (US$1.1 billion) to defense over the next three years, with expenditures of some Can$11.2 billion (US$7.5 billion) in 2001–2002. The bulk of this money will go to equipment upgrades and purchases, training and quality-of-life initiatives, and payments for operations in Kosovo and East Timor.

In 2000, the Canadian navy took delivery of the first of four Victoria (former Upholder)-class diesel-electric submarines from the United Kingdom. In addition, the first of 15 new search-and-rescue helicopters will be delivered in 2001, and delivery of light armored vehicles and reconnaissance vehicles has continued. Canada's CF18 fighter fleet is also undergoing modernization. Despite these developments, important equipment categories of the Canadian military are aging. In particular, new maritime helicopters to replace the 30-year-old Sea King fleet are needed. The modernization of maritime patrol aircraft, improved airlift and sealift assets, new fleet replenishment vessels, and modern military satellite communications systems are priorities as well.

CONTRIBUTIONS TO REGIONAL AND GLOBAL SECURITY

GLOBAL SECURITY   Canada sought to utilize its seat on the UN Security Council (1999–2000), particularly during the months it served as chair, to increase the council's transparency and to chair sessions on human security issues, including civilians in armed conflict, children in war and conflict zones, and the proliferation of small arms. Axworthy and Chrétien also emphasized these issues during the UN Millennium Summit and the fall 2000 meeting of the UN General Assembly. In addition, the Canadian ambassador to the United Nations was a key figure in producing a report on the role of diamonds in perpetuating the Angolan civil war.

Canada has maintained its engagement in 11 UN peacekeeping operations around the world. However, it has begun to take a more cautionary stance regarding new commitments. This reflects Canada's lack of resources and its insistence on more effective UN mission mandates and agreed-in-advance commitments of troops and funding.

REGIONAL SECURITY   Canadian officials have voiced disappointment at what they regard as the slow progress and reticence on the part of Asia Pacific multilateral institutions such as the ARF. Nonetheless, they have remained actively engaged in these institutions and have sought to motivate action on specific confidence-building measures and consideration of nontraditional security issues. The Canadian International Development Agency has also played a major role in funding unofficial cooperation projects, including the annual Asia Pacific Round Table in Kuala Lumpur, various ASEAN Institutes for Strategic and International Studies activities (including the ASEAN People's Summit of November 2000), and the Northeast Asia Cooperation Program, a recently established program focused on Northeast Asia.

In Northeast Asia, Canada and Japan have cochaired the Council for Security Cooperation in Asia Pacific (CSCAP) North Pacific Working Group. This group continues to function as the only "full-house" security dialogue in Northeast Asia, benefiting from the regular participation of North Korean and Mongolian delegates. As a result of North Korean membership in the ARF, this group might also take on new dimensions. Certainly, the most notable bilateral event of Canada's engagement with Asia Pacific in 2000 concerned North Korea. After Canada's efforts to advance North Korea's engagement and inclusion in regional institutions over the past decade, Canadian observers anticipate the establishment of diplomatic relations early in 2001.

Canada's engagement of troops and naval support vessels in the East Timor operation marked the first time in many years that Canada's military was actively deployed in Asia. Equipping and delivering the Canadian contingent and operating in conjunction with regional militaries provided the Canadian forces with valuable experience. It also brought

Canadian Defense Minister Art Eggleton to the region, including visits to Australia, New Zealand, and East Timor in January 2000.

The Canadian navy has continued its program of regular ship visits to Asia, alternating between Southeast Asian and Northeast Asian tours. In 2000, Canadian vessels visited China, Japan, and South Korea. Moreover, a Chinese ship visited the Pacific Maritime Command in the summer of 2000, marking the first time a People's Liberation Army (PLA) vessel has come to Canada.

5 China

The People's Republic of China's (PRC's) economy developed better than expected in 2000. Its internal and external security environments remained stable as well. Although the change of leadership in Taiwan was not desirable in the view of the Chinese government, the situation has not turned into a crisis. In addition, relations with the United States, Russia, Japan, and Southeast Asian countries generally developed smoothly and were strengthened. Thus, China experienced an improvement in its external and internal security environment during 2000, laying the foundation for implementing further changes to the country's polity and economy in the first years of the new century.

INTERNAL   China's economic situation is better than had been expected. The economy grew at 8.2 percent in the first three quarters of 2000, and the growth rate for the whole year should exceed 8 percent. The Central Committee of the Communist Party of China (CPC), at its annual session in October, passed the proposal for the 10th Five-Year Plan covering 2001 to 2005. The plan calls for maintaining relatively rapid economic growth and implementing structural changes in the Chinese economy. The plan also emphasizes the development of science and technology, education, and the establishment of a new welfare system.

After weathering the Asian financial crisis of 1997–1999 relatively smoothly, China's economy should maintain high growth rates of between 7 percent and 8 percent and reach the objectives of the current Five-Year Plan. During this period, the Chinese economy should undergo not only quantitative changes but also qualitative changes, with the information and other high-technology sectors developing into major drivers of the economy. In addition, the country's western regions should see a boom in infrastructure development.

A strong economy will promote changes in other fields. The process of establishing a new social welfare system to cover retirement, unemployment, minimum income, and medical care benefits is likely to accelerate, promoting social stability in China's rapidly changing society. Smooth economic and social development will also provide an environment for the Chinese leadership to push political reform, which has been on the party's and the government's agenda for some time. Finally, China's entry into the World Trade Organization (WTO) has reached the final stage of multilateral negotiations, and China will very likely become a member of the WTO in 2001. Entry into the WTO will trigger fundamental changes in China's economy, society, and politics. WTO entry should promote the development of the rule of law both at the individual business level and also at the local and central government levels.

The election of Chen Shui-bian to the Taiwanese presidency was not a desirable development in the eyes of China's government, but so far it has not triggered highly increased tensions across the Taiwan Strait. When Chen was elected on March 18, the PRC's Taiwan Affairs Office issued a statement, stressing that the election of a new leader in Taiwan would never change the fact that Taiwan is a part of China. "Taiwan independence" in any form will never be allowed, the statement noted. But the statement also expressed flexibility, saying that the PRC is willing to exchange views on cross-Strait relations and peaceful reunification with all parties, organizations, and persons in Taiwan who favor the one-China principle. The statement also took a wait-and-see approach: "We should listen to what the new leader in Taiwan says and watch what he does. We will observe where he will lead cross-Strait relations."

After the election, China's leaders repeatedly insisted that the basis for cross-Strait negotiations and peaceful relations is the recognition of the one-China principle, stating that under this principle, "everything can be discussed." Beijing also called on Taiwan's new leadership to take substantial steps and to refrain from merely making gestures. Beijing regarded Chen's policies of "goodwill reconciliation" as lacking sincerity because Chen adopted an evasive, ambiguous attitude toward the one-China principle. Beijing further indicated that there would be no contact and dialogue with Taiwanese authorities and the Democratic Progressive Party, unless they accepted the one-China principle.

Meanwhile, trade, investment, and other economic activities across the Taiwan Strait continued to grow during the year. Taiwanese authorities commenced limited direct links in trade, transport, and postal services between two offshore islands, Kinmen and Matsu, and the mainland in January 2001.

EXTERNAL   China's relations with the United States improved during 2000, including the normalization of military-to-military ties. In late January, Lieutenant General Xiong Guangkai, deputy general chief of staff, led a six-member senior military delegation to the United States to resume bilateral military talks. This was the first formal high-level military contact between the two nations since the bombing of the Chinese Embassy in Belgrade in May 1999. The two countries also conducted mutual port calls by naval vessels and resumed talks on disarmament and weapons proliferation.

Sino-U.S. relations made two major breakthroughs in 2000. First, a bill granting permanent normal trade relations (PNTR) for China was passed by the U.S. Congress in September. Second, an agreement on missile transfers was reached in November. According to this agreement, China promises not to transfer missiles and missile technology to nations developing nuclear weapons. In exchange, the United States will lift sanctions levied against China due to the missile transfer issue. Other issues between the two countries remain, however, including U.S. arms sales to Taiwan, human rights, and missile defense.

Sino-Russian relations maintained strong positive momentum after President Vladimir Putin took office. Putin visited China in July. The two countries issued the Beijing Declaration and agreed to solidify their strategic partnership, promote a multipolar world, and build a new international order. China and Russia are also actively preparing to sign a general treaty on friendly cooperation in May–June 2001 when China's President Jiang Zemin is scheduled to visit Russia.

China tried to improve its relations with Japan during the year. Premier Zhu Rongji paid a six-day visit to Japan in October, talking with Japanese government leaders and business representatives and holding a televised town hall meeting with 100 Japanese citizens. Premier Zhu said during the visit that China wishes that Japan could play a bigger and more active role in international and regional affairs. He also said that China will cooperate with Japan to promote East Asian cooperation, taking concrete steps to advance progress. The two countries agreed to establish a hotline and to strengthen and expand dialogue on bilateral security issues. Finally, they agreed to increased military exchanges and navy visits.

However, the relationship with Japan also faces obstacles. The Chinese government reiterated its indignation at several "anti-China incidents," such as right-wing Japanese denying the Nanjing Massacre, Japanese Youth League activists setting foot on the Diaoyu/Senkaku Islands, and Japanese cabinet members visiting the Yasukuni Shrine. The two countries also disagreed over research in the East China Sea.

According to the Chinese, the dispute is a result of the two countries' inability to agree on the demarcation of boundary lines in the East China Sea. During a visit to China in August by Japanese Foreign Minister Kōno Yōhei, China and Japan agreed in principle that each side should inform the other about research in disputed waters. However, the Chinese stressed that research in the East China Sea is not unusual and conforms to international laws. Information exchange on East China Sea research should thus be considered as an independent act by each side and would not serve to alter China's position on the demarcation of boundary lines. In late September, the two countries held a first round of talks in Beijing to craft the specifics of an agreement and discuss a code of conduct regarding research in disputed waters.

One of the most positive events of the year was a breakthrough in Sino–North Korean relations when North Korea's leader Kim Jong Il paid a three-day visit to China in late May–early June. The trip was the first journey abroad by the North Korean leader since he succeeded his father in 1994. Discussions covered the two countries' relations and the international and regional situation. China declared that it supports North Korea's reunification policy and efforts to improve relations with the South, while North Korea supported China's position expressed in the Taiwan white paper. Following the visit, China sent a high-level military delegation led by the defense minister to North Korea in late October.

Sino–South Korean relations also experienced a breakthrough when Chinese Defense Minister Chi Haotian visited Seoul in January. This was the first time in five decades that China's defense minister had visited South Korea.

China's relations with India recovered somewhat during 2000. Indian President Kocheril Raman Narayanan visited China in May. The two countries agreed to increase economic exchanges and strengthen cooperation in international affairs to promote a "new world order." In July, Chinese Foreign Minister Tang Jiaxan visited India. The minister raised a five-point proposal for enhancing bilateral relations with India, covering the border issue, economic cooperation, military relations, and the two countries' security dialogue. On the border issue, Tang said that China has made positive proposals and believes that the process of checking and clarifying the middle sections of the Line of Actual Control should be accelerated. In addition, the Joint Working Group on the border issue should accelerate its work during the round of border talks that started in New Delhi in late April.

China saw its ties with Southeast Asian countries grow stronger in 2000. In October, China and the Association of Southeast Asian Nations (ASEAN) signed an agreement on anti-drug cooperation. In November, President Jiang visited Laos and Cambodia. During the same month, Premier Zhu attended the ASEAN+1 (China) dialogue meeting and the ASEAN+3 (China, Japan, and South Korea) meeting in Singapore and proposed several initiatives for promoting economic cooperation between China and Southeast Asia.

China's relations with Vietnam continued to improve. After the 1999 signing of an agreement on land territory, the two sides worked to reach an agreement on the demarcation of Beibu Bay before the end of 2000. Vietnam and China also expected to sign an agreement regarding the fishing industry within the year. Finally, during Vietnamese Prime Minister Phan Van Khai's visit to China in September, the two countries agreed to increase their economic relations, setting the goal of US$2 billion in bilateral trade for 2000.

China's relations with the Philippines encountered further problems during 2000. Several incidents occurred in the South China Sea. Early in the year, the Philippine navy boarded Chinese fishing vessels near the Huangyan shoal. China condemned this incursion and urged the Philippine government to respect China's territorial sovereignty over the Nansha Islands. On May 26, a Chinese fishing boat, after experiencing engine problems, drifted into waters off the Philippine island of Palawan. The Philippine maritime police pursued the boat and shot at it. One fisherman was killed, and seven others were detained but later allowed to return home with their boat. The Chinese government expressed shock and strong dismay to the Philippine government over this incident, and asked for compensation for the fisherman's death.

Despite these incidents, diplomatic efforts to resolve the South China Sea issue continued. During a visit by then Philippine President Joseph Estrada in May, President Jiang said that the most realistic approach

CHINA 55

would be cooperation in the exploration and development of disputed areas. In a joint statement signed during the visit, the two countries also agreed to promote a peaceful settlement and contribute to the formulation and adoption of a regional code of conduct in the South China Sea. Work to narrow differences on the code continued in a second round of ASEAN-China consultations in the northeastern Chinese city of Dalian in August.

DEFENSE POLICIES AND ISSUES

DEFENSE POLICY China's *Defense White Paper 2000* states that China maintains a small but effective nuclear deterrent. The white paper also reaffirms the Chinese government's support for the basic principle of "peaceful reunification under one country, two systems" for settling the Taiwan issue. However, the white paper states that if events occur that lead to the separation of Taiwan from China by any name, if Taiwan is invaded and occupied by foreign countries, or if Taiwanese authorities indefinitely refuse negotiations for a peaceful settlement of cross-Strait reunification, the Chinese government will have no choice but to adopt all possible measures, including the use of force.

In late February, the Chinese government also issued a white paper on the one-China principle and Taiwan issue. This white paper added that the mainland would use force if Taiwanese authorities indefinitely refuse to accept the one-China principle and national reunification. Beijing has so far adopted a "wait and see" position toward Taipei, waiting to see the attitude of the new leadership. This position is likely to continue for the foreseeable future.

DEFENSE SPENDING The official figure for defense spending for fiscal year 2000 is 120.5 billion yuan (US$14.5 billion at 1 yuan = US$0.12). This is a 12.7 percent increase over the previous year. The growth rate is similar to that of recent years, and the current increase is mainly to cover costs for salary increases and the stationing of troops in Macao. According to the *Defense White Paper 2000*, China's defense expenditure falls into three categories: personnel expenses, costs for maintenance of activities, and equipment costs. During fiscal 2000, as in other recent years, each of these categories took up roughly one-third of defense expenditures.

ORGANIZATIONAL CHANGE   At the end of March 2000, business operations affiliated with but not related to the functions of the army, the People's Armed Police, and law enforcement agencies were completely separated from these units. Announced in July 1998, the transition to independent business procedures is said to have proceeded smoothly and resulted in notable achievements.

MILITARY MODERNIZATION   At the 9th National People's Congress in March 2000, President Jiang urged the People's Liberation Army (PLA) to push modernization to a new level and enhance combat readiness and defense capabilities by using high technology. In addition, the realization of a reduction of 500,000 personnel by the end of 1999 is a sign that the PLA is making significant progress toward the goal of transforming itself into a lean, combined, and highly efficient force.

MISSILE DEFENSE   China continues to criticize U.S. efforts to establish national missile defense (NMD) and theater missile defense (TMD) systems. Speaking at the ASEAN Regional Forum (ARF) meeting in Bangkok in July, Foreign Minister Tang said the development of NMD and TMD will surely disrupt the global strategic balance and lead to a new arms race. This would have widespread negative influence on international efforts for peace, disarmament, and nonproliferation. The Chinese representative to the UN Disarmament Conference reiterated this position, stating that the development and deployment of NMD would undermine global stability and threaten international peace.

China also supports Russia's position that the integrity of the Anti-Ballistic Missile (ABM) Treaty must be maintained. The two countries issued a joint statement on ABM in July stressing that the plan to establish NMD is a cause for profound concern. The joint statement also said that a nonstrategic missile defense program and international cooperation in such areas, which are not prohibited by the ABM Treaty, should not undermine security interests of other countries, lead to the establishment of any closed military or political bloc, or threaten global and regional stability and security. The joint statement added: "The incorporation of Taiwan into any foreign missile defense system is unacceptable and will seriously undermine regional stability."

China's *Defense White Paper 2000* further elaborated China's stance, criticizing the joint research and development by the United States and Japan of a TMD system with a view to deploying it in East Asia. It said such efforts would enhance the overall offensive and defensive capabilities of the U.S.-Japan military alliance to an unprecedented level, far exceeding the defensive needs of Japan. China also strongly objects to the provision of TMD components, technology, or systems to Taiwan, emphasizing China's resolute opposition to attempts at incorporating Taiwan in any form in the TMD system.

ARMS CONTROL   China has linked its arms-control policy to America's missile defense program. Ambassador Sha Zukang, director-general of the Department of Arms Control and Disarmament at the Ministry of Foreign Affairs, said in April 2000 that recent profound changes, particularly actions by the United States, may force China to review its policies on a wide range of arms control and nonproliferation issues. He stressed that China will not sit back and watch its legitimate security interests being undermined without taking countermeasures. Sha said China's participation in arms control negotiations, particularly regarding nuclear weapons, is based on two conditions. First, "these negotiations and the treaties or agreements resulting from these negotiations must not undermine the global strategic balance and stability." And second, "China's important strategic security interests" must be protected.

China continues its support for the Comprehensive Test Ban Treaty (CTBT) and its early implementation. The Chinese government has formally submitted the CTBT to the National People's Congress, China's top legislature, for ratification. China also supports negotiations on a Fissile Material Cut-off Treaty. Finally, Chinese arms-control officials have said that preventing the introduction of outer space arms deserves more urgent attention and that substantive work should be carried out on this issue. China proposes that the prevention of an outer space arms race should be one of the top priorities of the UN Disarmament Conference and calls for an international treaty on the subject.

CONTRIBUTIONS TO REGIONAL AND GLOBAL SECURITY

KOREA   China strongly supports the rapprochement between North and South Korea. President Jiang hailed the successful inter-Korean summit as a major event of historical significance and sent letters to the leaders of both North and South Korea reiterating China's position that the situation on the Korean peninsula should be resolved through dialogue and negotiations. In China's view, the North-South summit has encouraged a relaxation of the security situation on the Korean peninsula and contributed to peace and stability in the Asia Pacific region. In addition, during Kim Jong Il's visit to China, China pledged to provide further grain and goods to aid North Korea in overcoming its difficulties.

EAST TIMOR   In 2000, China decided to give 50 million yuan (US$6 million) to East Timor to help the war-torn territory rebuild. Foreign Minister Tang announced this aid in January in a meeting in Beijing with visiting East Timor independence leader Jose Alexandre Xanana Gusmao. Tang said China respects the choice made by the East Timorese people, who voted overwhelmingly in August 1999 for independence from Indonesian rule. China is happy to see that the situation in East Timor has improved, aided by the efforts of the United Nations and East Timorese interests. Tang also confirmed that in addition to sending money, China would take the rare step of sending peacekeeping staff to work with UN authorities in East Timor. Ten Chinese police officers had already arrived in East Timor to join the UN transitional authority in January. Another 40 civilian police officers joined them in early September.

ASEAN REGIONAL FORUM   China continued to participate in ARF activities during 2000. Foreign Minister Tang attended the seventh ARF meeting in Bangkok in July. Tang praised the ARF's contribution to regional stability over the past six years, extolling the positive role that the forum has played as an operational mechanism enhancing dialogue, understanding, and cooperation. China also welcomed North Korea's first-ever participation in the ARF during 2000. In September, China hosted the fourth ARF meeting of the heads of defense colleges. Fifty-eight participants from 21 countries of the ARF and eight observers attended the meeting. The main topics of the seminar covered Asia Pacific security, enhancement of cooperation among defense colleges, and reinforcement of education in the information age. The meeting also discussed the situation on the Korean peninsula, Fiji, and the causes of regional conflicts. At the opening ceremony, Defense Minister Chi praised the ARF's positive role, saying that he believed the ARF is becoming the main channel for multilateral security dialogue and cooperation in the Asia Pacific region.

CENTRAL ASIA   The "Shanghai Five," comprising the leaders of China, Kazakhstan, the Kyrgyz Republic, Russia, and Tajikistan, held their annual summit meeting in Dushanbe, Tajikistan, in July. Originally formed to resolve border issues, this grouping has now shifted its focus to promoting cooperation in the political, economic, and security arenas. During the meeting, the five governments agreed to work together to guarantee regional security, crack down on religious extremism and ethnic separatism, and combat international terrorist activities. Cooperation on these issues was strongly supported and encouraged by China.

Earlier during the year in March, the "Shanghai Five" defense ministers met in Astana, Kazakhstan. A joint communiqué was signed supporting the ABM Treaty, a nonnuclear zone in Central Asia, and UN efforts in Afghanistan. The five ministers also pledged to further implement arms reduction and confidence-building measures among the five nations; to cooperate in disaster relief, peacekeeping, and joint military activities; and to fight drug trafficking, weapons smuggling, and international terrorism.

6 European Union

As in the preceding year, European security concerns in 2000 were dominated by events in the Balkans and by efforts to build a credible common capability for European power projection. Several security developments in Asia Pacific during the year were of relevance to Europe as well, however, including the hostage crisis in the southern Philippines, instability in Indonesia, events on the Korean peninsula, and the Asia-Europe Meeting (ASEM) held in Seoul.

In the Balkans, the political situation improved substantially during 2000. In Croatia, the pace of democratization accelerated after the death of its first president, Franjo Tudjman, and a change in power to the former opposition. As a consequence, Croatia shifted toward a much more cooperative relationship with both its neighbors and the European Union (EU). On October 5, 2000, efforts to rig the presidential election results in the Federal Republic of Yugoslavia triggered a popular revolt against the old regime of Slobodan Milosevic and led to the assumption of power by an opposition politician, Vojislav Kostunica, who rapidly moved to improve relations with other successor states of the former Yugoslavia, as well as with the West. He paid a state visit to Bosnia on October 22 and participated in a summit meeting of all southeast European states held in Macedonia on October 25. The West welcomed Serbia (the main republic in the Federal Republic of Yugoslavia) to the Stability Pact for South Eastern Europe, a comprehensive effort to stabilize and eventually integrate southeast Europe into Western institutions. Western nations also began to lift sanctions and extended promises of financial support to Serbia. Within Serbia, however, the change in power and the process of democratization is proceeding slowly and uncertainly.

Triggered by Europe's marginalization during the Kosovo war, European efforts to increase the capability for sustainable common military intervention accelerated in 2000, a pace expected to continue in 2001. These efforts focused on the so-called headline goals, which propose a common force of about 60,000 ground troops capable of long-distance power projection, deployable within 60 days and sustainable for one year or longer.

The European Union's drive to strengthen common foreign policy and security capabilities raises the possibility that Europe will be more willing to contribute to East Asian security in the future. Statements by the European Union's high representative, Javier Solana, seem to suggest a greater European enthusiasm to contribute to Asian security, especially peace building. Clearly, events in 2000 on the Korean peninsula, in the Philippines, and in East Timor illustrated that Europe cannot afford to ignore security developments in East Asia. Political instability in major Asian countries, such as Korea, Indonesia, and China, can easily threaten global economic and political stability, thus severely affecting European interests. Moreover, the export of technology for weapons of mass destruction or long-range missiles from East Asia to the Middle East or North Africa could directly influence the security balance in Europe's immediate surroundings.

However, the European Union's enthusiasm to strengthen security in East Asia has to be seen in perspective. While Europe has important and tangible security interests in East Asia, they are secondary, and Europe's military capabilities will, for the foreseeable future, be insufficient to play anything but a limited and subsidiary role in efforts to enhance East Asian regional stability. Consequently, Europe's principal contribution to regional security will continue to be nonmilitary and primarily economic. In fact, after emerging from the financial crisis of 1997, East Asia's economic relations with Europe recovered substantially during 2000.

DEFENSE POLICIES AND ISSUES

DEFENSE POLICIES   The Kosovo war exposed severe deficiencies in Europe's capacity for military crisis management, and thus propelled a serious push toward a common European defense and security policy.

Facilitated by the United Kingdom's change of heart in favor of European security and defense cooperation, the European Union made rapid progress in setting up the decision-making infrastructure for such a policy in 2000. By the end of the year, a political and security committee was established as the highest decision-making body, a military committee and military staff began working on practical steps toward the implementation of the "headline goals," and Solana, formerly the secretary-general of the North Atlantic Treaty Organization (NATO), assumed the position of EU High Representative for the Common Foreign and Security Policy (CFSP). Efforts to consolidate Europe's defense industries also continued. Particularly important in this respect was the decision during 2000 to develop a European long-distance military transport aircraft based on the Airbus.

In general, the CFSP seeks to give Europe the capabilities to project military power to deal with humanitarian emergencies, major peace-keeping operations, and military peace enforcement. While political momentum has continued to build toward establishing these capabilities, the ability of the European Union to realize its ambitions remains uncertain. In fact, the development of capabilities to project military power would require not only an extensive restructuring of European armed forces but also a substantial increase in defense spending. So far, European defense expenditures and restructuring efforts remain insufficient to fill critical gaps in long-range transport, surveillance, command, control, and communications.

The CFSP was conceived as an effort in intergovernmental cooperation. Thus, joint national efforts are critical to provide the building blocks. France and the United Kingdom early on initiated efforts to restructure their armed forces in line with the "headline goals." In 2000, Germany and Italy followed suit. Italy completely suspended conscription. Germany, on the other hand, announced plans to restructure its armed forces. Germany's armed forces had been geared toward fending off an attack by the Warsaw Pact forces from the east. Now, the Bundeswehr is to become a smaller, more versatile, and more effective fighting force, changing its orientation from territorial defense toward intervention and power projection. The Bundeswehr will also become a more professional force, with conscription retained, but at a very low level. The realization of these goals will take considerable time and may be complicated by a lack of available financial resources. Overall, Germany's foreign and security role as a "civilian power" that rules out unilateral power projection has been modified but not dissolved by these recent changes.

The new CFSP is also an issue of contention with the United States. The United States, while officially welcoming greater defense efforts by European allies, remains skeptical about Europe's willingness to strengthen its military capabilities. Since the CFSP seeks to project military power in cooperation with, but if necessary without, the United States, questions about the future of transatlantic security cooperation are raised as well. The United States has been wary about any tendency to develop European military capabilities outside the NATO framework and reluctant to accept a greater European role in security decision making within NATO.

Conversely, the U.S. intent to press ahead with national missile defense (NMD) and theater missile defense (TMD) programs is viewed with considerable misgivings in Europe. There is concern that such programs could complicate relations with Russia, ignite arms races, and, most seriously, lead toward "strategic decoupling" between the United States and Europe. Consequently, Europe's interest in TMD has so far been rather muted, even though Europe faces possible missile threats from the Middle East and North Africa.

In sum, Europe entered 2001 continuing its push toward a credible European military capability and security identity. However, many questions remain, notably whether European governments are willing to cede their cherished national defense autonomy, whether appropriate security relations can be arranged with the United States, and whether European countries are able to mobilize necessary financial resources.

DEFENSE BUDGETS For the whole of NATO Europe, defense expenditures in 1999 were slightly lower in real terms than in the previous year (see table 1), with few signs that this trend will be reversed in the near future. Moreover, due to the decline of the euro vis-à-vis the U.S. dollar, defense expenditures were substantially down in real dollar terms. In particular, Germany is likely to see a further decline in real defense spending, forcing the delay of vital arms procurement programs needed for Germany's contribution toward the common European defense effort. Among the major countries, only the United Kingdom has seen the post–cold war decline in defense spending bottom out.

Table 1. Defense Expenditures in the European Union

Country	1999 Defense Expenditure	% of GDP	1998 Defense Expenditure	% of GDP
France	US$37,893*	2.7	US$40,834	2.8
United Kingdom	36,876	2.6	38,093	2.7
Germany	31,117	1.6	33,802	1.5
Italy	22,046	2.0	23,934	2.0
Spain	7,263	1.3	7,522	1.3
Netherlands	6,964	1.8	7,192	1.8
NATO Europe	174,375	2.3	184,192	2.2

SOURCE: *Military Balance, 2000/2001*. London: International Institute for Strategic Studies, 2000.
*U.S. dollar figures are at constant prices for 1999.

CONTRIBUTIONS TO REGIONAL AND GLOBAL SECURITY

Over the last decade, Europe's involvement with Asia has grown both broader and deeper. This trend is likely to continue. The change in the European Union's foreign and security policy does not signify that Europe will assume key responsibilities for security and stability in the Asia Pacific region. Rather, an intensified security relationship between Europe and Asia enhances the resilience and diversity of regional and global interaction in Asia Pacific.

BILATERAL RELATIONS   During 2000, the most conspicuous security-related development between Europe and an Asian country concerned the hostage crisis in the southern Philippines. This crisis involved hostages from France, Germany, and Finland and underlined the salience of human security issues in diplomatic relations between Europe and East Asia. Eventually, the European hostages were freed, but only after a stream of high-ranking European diplomatic visits and ransom payments, arranged in part by Libya.

Another important event in the European Union's relations with East Asia during 2000 was the development of diplomatic relations by several EU members with North Korea. Sweden, as a neutral country, had long maintained a diplomatic presence in North Korea. In 2000, Belgium, Italy, Finland, and Portugal moved toward full diplomatic relations. Germany and the United Kingdom also announced decisions to do so shortly before the ASEM gathering in Seoul. France, however, which held the EU presidency in the second half of 2000, publicly opposed early recognition, thus demonstrating openly that the European Union was unable to agree on this issue.

After the ASEM gathering, the European Union held its third summit meeting with China. This summit brought together the presidency of the European Union (France), the European Commission, and the Chinese leadership. It underlined that relations with China dominate Europe's interest in Asia, overshadowing even relations with Japan. The EU-China summit was used to push for China's entry into the World Trade Organization (WTO) before the end of the year 2000.

The importance accorded China's WTO accession by the European Union underlines the fact that European bilateral relations with China are dominated by economic and commercial considerations. Other issues, such as China's human rights record, are secondary. Indeed, what Europe fundamentally lacks is a strategy that could address in a comprehensive way China's emergence as a global power. Even France's policy toward China, which occasionally appears to display signs of such a strategy, seems driven mainly by commercial considerations and France's own foreign policy agenda vis-à-vis the United States. It seems that Europe hopes a richer, more powerful China will turn out to be a benign great power. Thus, Europe's instincts are to draw China more closely into the fold of international institutions and economic exchange. However, no serious consideration is given to what Europe could and should do if its hopes turn out to be too optimistic.

ARMS SALES   As previously noted, European suppliers provided during the mid-1990s roughly one-fifth of the total East Asian arms market, with Indonesia, Malaysia, South Korea, and Taiwan the major customers. In the late 1990s, European arms sales to East Asia contracted sharply, affected by the Asian financial crisis and the completion of the largest recent arms deal between Europe and East Asia—the Taiwanese purchase of fighter aircraft and frigates from France. Europe's arms sales to East Asia began to recover in 2000, however. Korea decided on German technology to build a new generation of submarines in a contract worth some US$700 million, and France received a large order from Singapore for its Lafayette-class frigates.

DEPLOYMENTS IN ASIA PACIFIC   Only two EU members, the United Kingdom and France, have direct security ties in East Asia. The United Kingdom continues to be a member of the Five Power Defense Arrangements (FPDA) grouping with Australia, Malaysia, New Zealand, and Singapore. In addition, some 1,000 Gurkha troops are stationed in, and financed by, the sultanate of Brunei. France retains possessions in the South Pacific (French Polynesia, New Caledonia, and Wallis and Futuna) and maintains a permanent military presence in the region (support ships, aircraft, and helicopters in addition to 6,200 men and three frigates).

OFFICIAL DEVELOPMENT ASSISTANCE (ODA) The European Union accounts for about 60 percent of global ODA. The European Union is also, after Japan, the most important source of ODA to Asia Pacific. During 1997–1998, the last period for which comprehensive data are available from the Development Assistance Committee of the Organisation for Economic Co-operation and Development (OECD), the European Union contributed about 38 percent of total ODA to Asia Pacific. This represents a substantial increase over a decade earlier, both in absolute U.S. dollar terms (up almost 50 percent) and as a share of total ODA to Asia Pacific (up from 33 percent). Most of the European Union's ODA is disbursed through bilateral programs.

MULTILATERAL SECURITY While bilateral relations between Europe and Asia Pacific continue to be dominated by economic issues, both the European Union and several individual member states, chiefly France, Germany, Sweden, and the United Kingdom, maintain bilateral security dialogues. These dialogues serve to underpin the European Union's participation in multilateral security activities, especially the ASEAN Regional Forum (ARF), the Korean Peninsula Energy Development Organization (KEDO), and ASEM.

European participation in the ARF remains confined to the European Union itself, which normally is represented by the country holding the presidency. At the 2000 ARF meeting, the European Union was for the first time represented by the new CFSP troika. In the second half of 2000, this troika consisted of the EU presidency, represented by French Minister for Cooperation and Francophony Charles Josselin; High Representative for Common Foreign and Security Policy Solana; and European Commissioner for External Relations Christopher Patten. Although the CFSP chiefly focuses on Europe's security environment, the greater continuity and higher profile that the CFSP lends Europe's participation in the ARF could herald a more active European role in the future. The principal relevance of the 2000 ARF for Europe was the effort to relaunch the stalled EU-ASEAN dialogue. After a long hiatus caused by differences over East Timor and the participation of Myanmar in the dialogue, EU and ASEAN (Association of Southeast Asian

Nations) foreign ministers finally met again in late 2000 in Vientiane, Laos.

The European Union and a few individual member states participate in KEDO. The European Union contributed some US$65 million to KEDO from 1997 through the end of 2000 and holds one of KEDO's directorships. The European Union has also extended substantial humanitarian assistance to North Korea, both to alleviate human suffering and to contribute to stability on the Korean peninsula. Given the enduring financial troubles of KEDO, its principal sponsors—Japan, South Korea, and the United States—have sought a larger financial contribution from the European Union. Consequently, negotiations are under way over an increase in Europe's contribution.

From its inception, ASEM has, besides dialogues on economic and cultural affairs, encompassed a political and security dimension. Security discussions within ASEM focus on two particular aspects of security: global security concerns, such as weapons of mass destruction and UN peacekeeping operations; and human security issues, such as drug trafficking, organized crime, and the impact of warfare on children. At the time of the ASEM gathering held in Seoul in late October 2000, the summit was overshadowed by developments on the Korean peninsula, specifically the announcement of the Nobel Peace Prize for South Korean President Kim Dae Jung and the visit by U.S. Secretary of State Madeleine Albright to Pyongyang. The open split among Europeans on the issue of opening diplomatic relations with North Korea also detracted from the summit's agenda. Overall, the ASEM dialogue has acquired security content, though with little practical relevance for security in the Asia Pacific region.

Europe has been significantly involved in UN peacekeeping operations in East Asia, most recently in East Timor. A number of EU member countries, chiefly Portugal but also including Austria, Denmark, France, Spain, Sweden, and the United Kingdom, have contributed civilian and/or military personnel to the UN Transitional Administration in East Timor (UNTAET).

7 India

THE SECURITY ENVIRONMENT

After two years of comparative diplomatic isolation in 1998–1999, New Delhi today is a popular destination for government leaders from around the world. The world acknowledges India's prominent role in Information Technology (IT), and the country's economy remains robust with 6 percent growth per year. Nonetheless, India's regional environment remains tense. The development of nuclear weapons continues, though in a low-key manner, and overall defense expenditures are high and growing, with New Delhi substantially enhancing its military capabilities.

EXTERNAL ENVIRONMENT   India's international role and its responses to contemporary challenges are shaped by three overarching objectives: (1) to win international understanding and support for India's national interests; (2) to promote the cause of democracy and freedom; and (3) to develop broad-based cooperation with other countries, particularly with the permanent members of the UN Security Council and other major powers. Results in achieving these goals have been encouraging.

India has initiated strategic dialogues with France, Russia, and several other countries. Japanese Prime Minister Mori Yoshirō's visit to South Asia, including India, in August 2000 highlighted the growing economic ties between the two countries and the potential for cooperation in IT. Mori's visit followed a January 2000 visit by Indian Defense Minister George Fernandes to Japan. The chill in relations after the nuclear tests is now over. However, the resumption of Japanese Official

Development Assistance is contingent on India's signing the Comprehensive Test Ban Treaty (CTBT). During the year 2000, relations with the European Union (EU) also improved. An Indian delegation led by Prime Minister Behari Vajpayee attended a bilateral dialogue in Lisbon with EU representatives from Brussels and Prime Minister Antonio Guterres of Portugal, the country holding the EU presidency at the time.

Relations with the United States. A six-day visit by President Bill Clinton in March 2000, the first to India in 22 years by a U.S. president, was followed by Prime Minister Vajpayee's official visit in September to Washington. For the first time, the two largest democracies in the world are seriously engaged with each other and are beginning to co-operate meaningfully on economic issues such as investment, trade, and technology. The United States remains India's largest trading partner and the source of most of its foreign investment, with both trade and investments expected to grow even further in the coming years. Moreover, a sustained dialogue in a U.S.-Indian Joint Working Group on counterterrorism has been initiated, and two meetings between senior officials have already taken place.

Relations with Russia. President Vladimir Putin's visit to India on October 2–5, the first by a Russian president in seven and a half years, was another landmark event. Though Putin's visit was not as extensively covered in the media as Clinton's visit, it perhaps yielded more substantial results. A Declaration of Strategic Partnership was signed laying down the broad contours of mutual relations in the 21st century. In addition, 15 bilateral agreements were signed to enhance cooperation in legal, economic, military, and scientific matters. Finally, agreement was reached to hold annual summit meetings. The economic content of Indian-Russian relations continues to be low, however, with annual trade only about half of the former level with the entire Soviet Union. The main focus of New Delhi's engagement with Moscow is based on a strong arms supply and technology transfer relationship, which seems likely to develop further over the next decade.

Relations with China. India's relations with China improved in 2000, continuing the positive tone established during Foreign Minister Jaswant Singh's visit to Beijing in June 1999. President K. R. Narayanan paid a state visit to China in mid-2000 and high-level visits have continued, paralleling the years before the South Asian nuclear tests. The border areas remain largely peaceful and both sides have reiterated their adherence to the provisions of existing joint agreements. The two countries are committed to expediting progress on outstanding issues through Joint Working Groups and Expert Groups. However, the core issue of demarcating the common border in the Himalayas remains unresolved, with little progress to show. India has also noted the test firing of China's DF-31 and laboratory tests of DF-41 intercontinental ballistic missiles and is concerned about the likely presence in the Indian Ocean in the near future of SSBNs (Sub-surface Ballistic Nuclear, or nuclear-powered ballistic missile submarines) belonging to the People's Liberation Army. Meanwhile, two Indian naval ships, the destroyer *Delhi* and the corvette *Kora*, conducted goodwill visits to Shanghai and carried out joint exercises in September 2000.

Relations with Pakistan. Pakistan remains India's major security concern. In New Delhi's view, Pakistan is actively encouraging terrorism and waging a proxy war against India in Jammu and Kashmir. The level of violence has been rising. Indian security forces suffered nearly 400 fatalities in the province, and suicide squads modeled after those used in Palestine appeared during the year. A profound fear exists that Pakistan is emerging as an epicenter of Islamic fundamentalism. Thus, violence in Kashmir is seen as the manifestation of a deeper malaise.

New Delhi remains committed to finding a peaceful resolution and to preventing the situation from escalating into a larger war. As a gesture of goodwill, India announced on November 19, 2000, the cessation of all actions against terrorists for the Muslim holy month of Ramadan; the cessation was later extended another month to January 26, 2001. Pakistan responded by announcing a cease-fire along the Line of Control and later declared a partial unilateral pullback of forces from disputed border areas. These measures have substantially reduced violence and raised the prospects for a dialogue between all parties. For the first time in a decade, cautious hope for a possible end to the conflict has appeared.

India believes that Pakistan's nuclear arsenal is now even more firmly under military control and that Pakistan continues with weapon acquisitions well beyond its legitimate security interests. These factors clearly will influence India's own military planning. An arms race is thus emerging in the region and is likely to escalate, perhaps expanding to include China in the near future.

Relations with Other Neighbors. In the year 2000, India's attention was increasingly directed toward West Asia. India obtains much of its energy from West Asia, trade with this region exceeds US$10 billion a year, and large foreign currency remittances from Indian workers continue to be important for the Indian economy. Hence, India is concerned that the breakdown of the peace process between Israel and Palestine and the continuing Iraq-U.S./UN standoff might erupt once again into intraregional conflict threatening India's energy security.

There are also wider concerns in India regarding Central Asia. New Delhi remains committed to the unity, sovereignty, and territorial integrity of Afghanistan. India recognizes the Northern Alliance and is highly concerned about the Taliban government in Afghanistan with its established links to worldwide terrorism, especially its support of Islamic militants in Jammu and Kashmir. Clearly, India would like to see Central Asia remain peaceful, stable, and free from radical Islamic influences.

In India's immediate neighborhood, relations with Bangladesh, Bhutan, the Maldives, Myanmar, Nepal, and Sri Lanka remain stable and are perhaps better than they have been in some time. Even while maintaining its moral support for Myanmar's notable opposition leader, Aung San Suu Kyi, India sustains diplomatic relations with the State Peace and Development Council (SPDC) in Yangon. Official cooperation with Myanmar has increased in a number of areas, as demonstrated by the high importance accorded to the visit by SPDC Vice-Chairman General Maung Aye to India in November 2000. Detailed discussions were held on the countries' mutual security interests and the development of economic ties. Undoubtedly, one factor prodding India's engagement with Myanmar has been China's influence over the SPDC.

On the economic front, a free trade agreement came into effect with Sri Lanka beginning in March 2000. Another agreement is being finalized with Bangladesh. Borders between India and Nepal and Bhutan are open. India has reiterated its commitment to the unity of Sri Lanka and remains ready to facilitate negotiations to end the civil war in that country. Yet, regional cooperation through the South Asian Association for Regional Cooperation (SAARC) remains stalled. The annual summit meeting scheduled in Kathmandu in November 1999 was not held, due to Indian pressure to exclude Pakistan's military-ruled government. An early resumption of the overall SAARC process seems unlikely, though a senior officers' meeting was held in Colombo during November 2000.

Relations with Southeast Asia. Southeast Asia's importance for India's strategic interests was demonstrated by the "Look East" policy developed by New Delhi in the early 1990s. This policy was an attempt to move away from the Islamic countries to India's west and take part in the economic dynamism of East Asia. India has been an active participant in the ASEAN Regional Forum (ARF) since 1996 and has also been involved since 2000 in the track-two process through its full membership on the Council for Security Cooperation in Asia Pacific

(CSCAP). India's president visited Singapore and the foreign minister went to Vietnam in November 2000; both visits focused on regional cooperation. Yet, India has long been trying to enter the Asia-Pacific Economic Cooperation (APEC) forum, without success. India's engagement with Southeast Asia is thus still uneven, with New Delhi especially concerned about developments in Indonesia that have the potential to impact Indian security interests.

INTERNAL ENVIRONMENT   After five turbulent years, there is every prospect of political stability in the country. If Prime Minister Vajpayee's health remains strong, the centrist coalition government may well last its full five-year term until 2004. This would bring continuity to policies and enable the introduction of further economic liberalization measures.

However, India's internal security environment has shown no improvement in the last year. Although the cease-fire with the largest insurgent group in the Nagaland region continues to hold with only minor infringements, northeast India remains in the grip of ethnic insurgencies. Several groups are active in the region and sporadic outbreaks of violence have been reported in Assam. Elsewhere in the country major law and order problems persist, mostly due to the lack of effective governance and continued economic deprivation. This trend is likely to continue in the near term.

Finally, with the sudden rise of world oil prices, India's energy security has emerged as a major concern. India continues to be dependent on imports for about 70 percent of its energy needs. With a growing economy, this dependence is likely to increase in the near future. Attempts to secure future energy needs include developing mutually beneficial arrangements with neighbors to the east, protecting the country's inland oil infrastructure, securing international high seas transit, and exploiting resources on India's continental shelf.

DEFENSE POLICIES AND ISSUES

THE KARGIL INQUIRY   The May 1999 Kargil conflict, in which Indian forces repelled at high cost an infiltration of Pakistani regulars with intense, conventional combat across the Line of Control in Jammu and Kashmir, prodded the formation of an Inquiry Committee. This committee submitted its report to the government in early 2000. It was later placed before Parliament and made public. The report severely criticized the country's external intelligence establishment for lapses, although it exonerated the military hierarchy and intelligence organizations. Subsequently, four more high-level committees were established by the government to investigate various aspects of national security. The reports of these committees have been submitted and were being examined by the government at the end of 2000. These reports could possibly lead to major organizational, systemic, and procedural changes, including revamping the intelligence system, changing top military command structures, strengthening communications, augmenting the surveillance of high-altitude borders, and undertaking some new military procurements.

DRAFT NUCLEAR DOCTRINE   India's nuclear policy is based on the following principles, frequently articulated at the highest quarters of government:
- Maintenance of an effective and credible nuclear deterrent at a minimum level;
- A formal commitment to no first use of nuclear weapons;
- A unilateral moratorium on explosive nuclear tests;
- Negotiations at the Conference on Disarmament on a treaty banning the production of fissile material;
- An effective export control mechanism to prevent unauthorized transfer of sensitive equipment and technologies; and
- Assurance that the nuclear deterrent remains under strict political and civilian control.

In August 1999, a draft nuclear doctrine was submitted to the government by the National Security Advisory Board. It visualized a triad of delivery systems consisting of surface, air, and undersea launch components, with the likely total number of nuclear warheads estimated at around 150. However, very little has been heard about the doctrine's implementation. Lack of progress in developing practical nuclear capabilities has been chiefly due to resource constraints and a lack of necessary technology. In fact, the capabilities suggested by the draft doctrine are likely to take a number of years to acquire, although on August 20, 2000, India's defense minister authorized production of 300 nuclear-capable Prithvi missiles with a range of 150–250 kilometers.

Throughout the year 2000 there was a debate within India's government on the need for further nuclear testing. The prime minister, the foreign minister, and the national security advisor have firmly committed India to no further testing and to adherence to the CTBT even without India's signature on the treaty. Yet, the nuclear scientific community outside the government generally feels that there may be a need for additional tests in order to ensure the reliability of the nuclear arsenal and to validate new bomb designs. These arguments are likely to guarantee that India abstains from signing the CTBT for some years.

DEFENSE BUDGET   India's defense budget received a hefty boost following the Kargil conflict. An increase of more than 28 percent was approved over the previous year's budget (see table 1), not including the supplementary budget submitted later in 1999. This increase was mainly

Table 1. India's Defense Budget (in billions of rupees)

	1997–1998	1998–1999	1999–2000	2000–2001
Army	184	228	284	323
Air Force	91	92	104	145
Navy	48	62	70	82
Research and development	19	23	27	31
Defense production	11	7	0	4
Total	353	412	485	585

SOURCE: Indian Ministry of Defense Annual Report presented to the Parliament in late February 2000.
NOTE: The approximate exchange rate when the budget was submitted at the end of February 2000 was Rs 43.50 = US$1.

to make up for losses incurred in the conflict and to support increased troop deployment and surveillance of the high-altitude border area. The budget does not include accretions to meet the requirements of the draft nuclear doctrine or recently contemplated purchases from Russia. The rising trend in defense expenditure is likely to continue well into the future, though perhaps in smaller increments than this year.

DEFENSE ACQUISITIONS   India is currently embarking on a significant arms acquisition program, mainly from Russia, though with a continuing effort at diversification. The more prominent examples of diversification are the British jet trainer Hawk, additional purchases of French Mirage 2000D fighters, South African LIW 155-mm guns for the Arjun tank, and upgrading the 130-mm M-46 field gun to 155-mm caliber with Israeli assistance.

From Russia, the army is acquiring 310 T-90S tanks to replace the older Vijayanta and make up for the production shortfall in the indigenous Arjun tanks. Of the T-90S tanks, 124 will be imported directly from Russia and the remaining 186 will be delivered in a knocked-down state and assembled in India. The "Smerch" Multiple Launch Rocket System may also be acquired for the artillery.

Naval acquisitions will center on the aircraft carrier *Admiral Gorsh-kov* with MiG-29 carrier-based fighters. The carrier will replace the decommissioned *INS Vikrant* and make the Indian navy once more a two-carrier fleet with blue-water naval capability by the year 2010. The *Gorshkov* is a gift, but the costs of making extensive repairs and equipping the carrier are likely to come to well over US$1 billion. Detailed negotiations are in progress. The other major expenditure is the ongoing refitting of eight Kilo-class and four German HDW-class submarines. These are likely to come re-equipped with Club-S cruise missiles.

The air force is acquiring an additional long-range multirole combat aircraft, the Sukhoi 30 Mk 1 from Russia. Fifty were ordered in 1996 and in 1998 and are currently being supplied. A contract was signed on December 28, 2000, for the supply of additional Sukhoi 30 Mk 1 aircraft, including the manufacturing under license of 140 aircraft at Hindusthan Aeronautics in Bangalore. This contract is worth more than US$3 billion, making it the largest single defense purchase agreement for India and possibly also for Russia. In addition, a total of more than 100 MiG-21 fighters are undergoing major upgrades to prolong their service life. Two Russian A-50/Il-76 AWACS planes have been leased recently. And 40 Mi 17-1B transport helicopters are under purchase to support the Indian army's high-altitude operations.

CONTRIBUTIONS TO REGIONAL AND GLOBAL SECURITY

REGIONAL SECURITY   India continues to be engaged in developing regional cooperation, particularly in Southeast Asia. This occurs mainly through multilateral organizations such as the ARF and two initiatives partly led by India: the Indian Ocean Rim Association for Regional Cooperation (IOR-ARC) and the Bangladesh-India-Myanmar-Sri Lanka-Thailand Economic Cooperation (BIMSTEC) grouping. However, little progress was made in the latter two organizations during 2000.

UN PEACEKEEPING OPERATIONS   India has traditionally been one of the leading contributors to UN peacekeeping operations around the world and particularly in Asia and Africa, while abstaining from enforcement operations as a matter of principle. Over the years, 94 Indian soldiers have been killed in UN peacekeeping operations. At present,

India contributes a battalion group of about 800 officers and soldiers to the UN Interim Force in Lebanon (UNIFIL). A contingent of 20 army officers serves as military liaison officers in the Congo. Nearly 2,000 soldiers are deployed with the UN Armistice Mission in Sierra Leone (UNAMSIL), with the force commander also from India. The UNAMSIL operations proved particularly difficult. After rebel forces reneged on the accord, a large group of Indian peacekeepers was surrounded for several weeks. The group was rescued without a single casualty in a highly professional military operation launched by the Indian contingent.

India considers the UN Security Council's response to the Sierra Leone crisis as less than effective, leaving India with no option but to withdraw its forces, including the force commander. The date for this was set for November 2000 with two months' notice. At the same time, New Delhi stated that it remains ready and willing to provide troops to other UN peacekeeping operations should there be a request.

India has also expressed serious reservations to the United Nations concerning the current trend in international peacekeeping operations under the Security Council. Its permanent representative in New York has said that the Security Council tends to stretch its mandate well beyond its charter without adequately taking the views of the developing world into account. Clearly, India is against the tendency toward increased and unilateral humanitarian intervention, especially without Security Council mandates.

ARMS CONTROL   India remains committed to nondiscriminatory and universal nuclear disarmament. It is an active participant in the Conference on Disarmament in Geneva and at the United Nations Disarmament Commission (UNDC) in New York. As an original party to the Chemical Weapons Convention (CWC), India has discharged its responsibilities fully and faithfully. India is also actively participating in current discussions to strengthen the Biological and Toxic Weapons Convention.

The issues of antipersonnel land mines (APMs) and small arms and light weapons proliferation have also been of major concern to India. New Delhi is a party to Protocol II of the Inhumane Weapons Convention and has ratified the Amended Protocol II on Landmines and Protocol IV on Blinding Laser Weapons. India has proposed a complete ban on the use of APMs in situations other than "international armed conflict." On small arms proliferation, India, as a victim state, is actively engaged in the search for an effective solution.

8 Indonesia

The Security Environment

As Indonesia enters the year 2001, it is evident that many of the security problems encountered during 2000 will continue to inhibit Indonesia's economic and political recovery. Internally, the Indonesian government faces tremendous difficulties in overcoming security challenges ranging from secessionist movements, political uncertainties, and religious conflicts to a series of bomb explosions in Jakarta. Externally, the slow progress in solving the residual problems emanating from the East Timor saga, specifically how to deal with pro-Indonesian militias and refugees, is putting a strain on Indonesia's relations with the outside world, mainly with Western countries.

INTERNAL ENVIRONMENT *Fragile Economic Recovery.* Despite continuing political uncertainties, nervous markets, and fragile domestic and international confidence, Indonesia's economy in 2000 showed signs of recovery. Gross domestic product rose by 4.13 percent in the second quarter, compared to only 0.5 percent during the same period in 1999. Between January and September, the inflation index was 4.65 percent, and exports reached US$34.8 billion, growing by 19.6 percent compared to the same period in 1999. By the end of September, Indonesia's foreign reserves had increased to US$28.09 billion.

Economic conditions remained highly uncertain and volatile, however. The rupiah fluctuated and weakened to about Rp9,600 to the U.S. dollar at the end of the year. In terms of foreign investment, Indonesia was the only Asian country that experienced a net outflow of investment funds during 2000. By October, Indonesia's foreign debt had increased to approximately US$150 billion (91 percent of GDP), including about US$70 billion owed by the private sector. While the bank recapitalization program is nearly complete, Indonesia's ailing banking system will need a decade to fully recover and will require US$70 billion in government bailout funds. In short, the prospects for Indonesia's economy in 2001 remain highly uncertain.

Political Uncertainties. Indonesia began 2000 with a degree of optimism following the election of Abdurrahman Wahid as Indonesia's fourth president at the end of 1999. But this optimism quickly waned. Both Wahid's supporters and detractors began to express criticisms, resentments, and disappointments concerning the president's erratic style of decision making. Six months after his election, it became increasingly evident that Wahid's government faced serious problems in implementing policies and delivering on promises. Indeed, by the end of 2000, domestic confidence in President Wahid's government was at a low ebb.

Intra-elite tensions constituted another major feature of Indonesia's national politics during 2000. Three main issues were paramount. First, the president's relationship with the leaders of Islamic political parties, which had supported his election to the presidency, rapidly deteriorated. Second, Wahid's eccentric behavior also created new tensions between the president and his vice-president, Megawati Sukarnoputri. Third, despite initial successes in reducing the role of the military, tensions between the president and elements of the Indonesian National Military (TNI, Tentara Nasional Indonesia) continued to generate speculation about possible coup attempts.

Despite the growing divisions among political elites, President Wahid survived possible removal at the First Annual Session of the People's Consultative Assembly (MPR, Majelis Permusyawaratan Rakyat) in August. Relations between the president and Parliament have been continually strained, however. A parliamentary committee launched investigations into the president's possible involvement in several corruption cases, and Wahid was severely criticized and even threatened with impeachment. It is clear that the country's internal politics will remain volatile. Talk of impeachment will continue in 2001.

Secessionist Movements and Religious Conflicts. During 2000, the province of Aceh posed a serious challenge to the central government. At the beginning of the year, an opportunity for a political solution seemed to open when Indonesia's government and the Free Aceh Movement (GAM, Gerakan Aceh Merdeka) agreed to hold talks. These talks led to an agreement on May 12 to initiate a three-month truce, called a "humanitarian pause." The agreement, however, did not stop the violence. The situation was even compounded due to the possible involvement of military elements.

The extension of the "humanitarian pause" for another three months after it initially expired in September also failed to yield significant improvements in Aceh's security situation. Armed clashes, mysterious killings, and kidnappings continue to devastate the province. Further, it remains unclear how the central government could resolve the problem. Beyond an offer of wide-ranging autonomy, it appears that the Wahid administration has no other strategy for satisfying Acehnese grievances. Meanwhile, the Acehnese have clearly stated that a meaningful solution cannot be reached unless the government in Jakarta is prepared to address gross violations of human rights committed by the TNI during 1990–1998.

While the Aceh problem is still far from resolution, the secessionist challenge in the province of Irian Jaya (Papua) in the eastern part of the country has intensified. In June, a West Papuan National Congress held in Jayapura declared that the province would seek independence from the Republic of Indonesia. The central government predictably dismissed the declaration as illegal, and the TNI maintained that it was prepared to undertake military measures if needed. The security situation further worsened in early October when a riot erupted in Wamena after police tried to take down separatist flags. Papuans attacked migrant residents in the area, leaving 22 migrants and six indigenous Irianese dead; many others were wounded. Overall, the government has yet to devise a coherent strategy to deal with growing separatist aspirations, and it is not clear whether the scheduled implementation of a new regional autonomy bill in January 2001 will help reduce tensions in Irian Jaya.

The security situation in Maluku also showed no significant improvements during 2000. Bloody clashes between Muslims and Christians continued, and the government's inability to bring an end to the conflict raised frustrations on all sides. The security situation was further complicated when the security apparatus—both the military and the police—began to take part in the conflict by siding either with Muslims or Christians. Fortunately, the situation had calmed somewhat by the end of the year, although sporadic violence and armed clashes persist and serve as reminders that another cycle of violence is possible.

Role of the Military. The most significant development in Indonesia's politics since the election of President Wahid has been the military's diminished influence. After the removal of General Wiranto from the cabinet in early 2000, President Wahid moved rapidly to bring more discipline to, and assert greater civilian control over, the TNI. Wahid also appointed general officers loyal to him to key positions in the TNI leadership. The president's efforts appeared to have paid off significantly when, on April 21, Commander-in-Chief Admiral Widodo Adisutjipto submitted the result of an annual two-day military leadership meeting to the president, conveying the TNI's decision to finally relinquish its social and political functions (*dwi fungsi*). However, it remains to be seen whether this historic decision will actually be implemented.

Indeed, toward the end of 2000 the military appeared to have consolidated its position both vis-à-vis the president and reformist elements within its own ranks. In April, President Wahid appointed Lieutenant-General Agus Wirahadikusuma, a figure perceived by the public as a strong advocate of reform within the TNI but disliked by many in the TNI leadership, as chief of the Army Strategic Reserve Command (KOSTRAD). In August, however, the president was forced to remove Wirahadikusuma from his position. A group of generals, apparently disturbed by Wirahadikusuma's sharp criticisms of the TNI and his attempts to expose corruption cases within KOSTRAD, argued that the general had violated the military's "code of conduct" and upset the "internal system" of the TNI. In October, an effort by President Wahid to appoint General Wirahadikusuma as army chief-of-staff again was blocked by strong opposition from TNI generals.

These events demonstrate that the TNI remains a major factor in Indonesia's internal politics and that its bargaining position vis-à-vis the civilian president is growing. Further evidence of this trend was the decision by the MPR in August to extend the military's allotment of 38 seats appointed in the MPR, previously scheduled to be ended in 2004, until 2009. This move was criticized by reformers as an impediment to meaningful democratization and was also seen as demonstrating a lack of confidence in Indonesia's civilian leaders.

EXTERNAL ENVIRONMENT *Regional Developments.* Indonesia's perceptions of external threat did not change significantly in 2000. The protracted economic crisis confirmed Indonesia's dependence on international forces, especially the International Monetary Fund (IMF), the World Bank, and the United States. Such dependence on external forces raised suspicions toward the outside world among segments of Indonesia's society, particularly the political elite. Concerns expressed included the possible involvement of foreign countries in the regional rebellions of Aceh and Irian Jaya and in the religious clashes in Maluku. Many saw this foreign pressure as evidence of an international conspiracy to undermine Indonesia's stability and security.

The possibility of Indonesia's disintegration remains a source of anxiety in East and Southeast Asia. This anxiety prompted Indonesia's partners within the Association of Southeast Asian Nations (ASEAN) to express strong support for Indonesia's territorial integrity at their annual meeting in July. In addition, regional countries also expressed worries about the impact of Indonesia's protracted crisis on the security of major sea lanes, particularly the Strait of Malacca. In October, the Piracy Reporting Centre in Malaysia reported that incidents of piracy in the Strait of Malacca had increased, with most incidents occurring in Indonesian waters. With continuing political instability in Indonesia, piracy in the Strait of Malacca may hit a ten-year high.

East Timor and Relations with Australia. Even though it has been a year since East Timor's historic vote to separate from Indonesia, the territory continues to affect Indonesia's relations with the outside world. More than 120,000 East Timorese remain in refugee camps in West Timor, with Jakarta moving very slowly to address this problem. Differences within the government, especially within the TNI, on how to deal with pro-Indonesian militias in East Timor complicate this problem. The seriousness of this issue was highlighted when a mob killed three aid workers from the UN High Commissioner for Refugees on September 6 in Atambua. Pro-Jakarta militias were widely believed to be involved in the attack. The UN resolution passed subsequent to this incident forced Indonesia's government to take more concerted action to disarm the militias. Despite the arrest of one militia leader in October, however, the international community continues to express dissatisfaction with Indonesia's performance.

Indonesia's relations with Australia, which deteriorated rapidly after Canberra took the leading role in the international force in East Timor, appeared to improve slightly in 2000. After a number of meetings between President Wahid and Prime Minister John Howard, the government-to-government relationship seemed to progress. However, a meaningful recovery was still prevented by resistance from the Indonesian Parliament and political forces. In May 2000, President Wahid was forced to postpone a planned trip to Canberra due to strong domestic opposition, and another visit was thwarted by the Parliament in July. Many Indonesian politicians maintained that a visit to Australia by Wahid was appropriate only after Australia's prime minister visited Indonesia.

Resenting the United States and the World. Indonesia's relations with the United States also showed strains during 2000 and toward the end of the year deteriorated further. Indonesian leaders were particularly angered by what they perceived as growing American interference in Indonesia's domestic affairs. In the aftermath of the Atambua incident, U.S. Secretary of Defense William Cohen warned Indonesia that international financial institutions could not continue their assistance unless the militia problem in East Timor was resolved. Such blunt warnings were seen as threats and provoked angry reactions in Jakarta. Toward the end of the year, it seemed that the United States had gradually replaced Australia as the main target of resentment and anger for Indonesia's political elites and society.

Expressions of anger against the outside world were not limited to Australia and the United States. Elements within Indonesia's civilian and military elites also expressed resentment against the United Nations, especially after a UN resolution demanded that the Indonesian government investigate the Atambua incident and disarm pro-Jakarta militias. In addition, plans to send a UN investigative mission to Atambua were announced. The United Nations was criticized in Indonesia for being unfair, because Indonesia alone was blamed for the Atambua incident. Many, including key government officials, even suggested that foreign forces orchestrated the incident to embarrass and discredit Indonesia. There were also accusations that the incident was intended to cover up the failure of the United Nations to solve growing postindependence problems within East Timor.

DEFENSE POLICIES AND ISSUES

STRATEGIC PRIORITIES   Indonesia's defense strategy and priorities remain on the defensive and focused on internal developments. Throughout 2000, the military was preoccupied with maintaining domestic stability, countering insurgency movements, restoring its tarnished image, and accelerating internal consolidation. In enforcing internal order, the military played a secondary role to the police. During 2000, the TNI's attempt to restore its image suffered serious difficulties, especially due to the involvement of the military in a series of bombings in Jakarta. Military reform also moved slowly with no significant steps taken in

2000 beyond those already carried out in 1999. The only notable progress was the decision by President Wahid in July to remove the national police from the Ministry of Defense and put it under the presidency.

SPENDING AND PROCUREMENT Despite growing calls for professionalism, Indonesia's military still experienced budgetary problems. In 2000, the government allocated 7.7 percent of its budget for defense, only 1.3 percent of the country's GDP. The figure was sufficient to cover only approximately 25 percent to 30 percent of actual military needs. During 2000, however, there was an important shift in the allocation of the budget in which, for the first time, the largest share (35 percent) was given to the national police rather than to the army (33.1 percent). For fiscal year 2001, the government proposed an increase of 11.7 percent in the military budget. The largest segment, around Rp5.5 trillion (US$572.9 million at US$1 = Rp9,600)—out of a total proposed budget of Rp8.55 trillion (US$890.6 million)—is earmarked for salaries and welfare.

The continuation of the military embargo imposed by the United States poses a serious problem for the TNI in maintaining its operational capabilities. According to the former minister of defense, Juwono Sudarsono, the operational capabilities of the TNI decreased by 50 percent due to the embargo. Ironically, the air force and the navy suffered most, despite the fact that these two services were relatively free from charges of human rights violations. To overcome its predicament, the government began to explore the possibility of reducing its dependence on military supplies from Western countries. By mid-2000, Indonesia had commenced arms sales negotiations with China, Russia, and South Korea. Due to a serious lack of financial resources, however, no new major purchases were made until October 2000.

DEFENSE COOPERATION The Wahid government's slow reaction to activities by pro-Indonesian militias and postelection violations of human rights in East Timor seriously affected Indonesia's defense cooperation with the United States and Australia. Thus, the 1999 suspension of Australian and U.S. military relations with Indonesia remained in force. The United States also suspended all arms sales to Indonesia and blocked Indonesians from attending programs at federally funded military institutions.

Despite these difficulties, the United States began to take measured steps to resume bilateral military ties with Indonesia in early May.

Preliminary military-to-military contacts, however, continued to ex-clude the army, focusing instead on the Indonesian navy and air force. The Indonesian air force, for example, was invited to observe the Co-bra Gold exercise in Thailand, conducted in early May, that involved Singaporean, Thai, and U.S. forces. The Indonesian air force sent ten observers to the event. In September, Indonesia's navy took part in a bilateral exercise with the U.S. navy, CARAT-VI/2000 (Cooperation Afloat Readiness and Training), in the Bali Strait and on Asembagus and Surabaya. The exercise, involving naval landing vessels and ma-rines, was designed to train forces in providing humanitarian assistance in a disaster relief operation. However, in the aftermath of the Atambua incident in September, the U.S. Senate's Foreign Relations Committee passed a bill that extended the suspension of all U.S. military relations with Indonesia.

CONTRIBUTIONS TO REGIONAL AND GLOBAL SECURITY

Indonesia's active contribution to regional and global security in 2000 decreased significantly compared to the previous year. At the regional level, this was clearly demonstrated by the absence of Indonesia's For-eign Minister Alwi Shihab at both the ASEAN Regional Forum (ARF) and the ASEAN+3 (ASEAN plus China, Japan, and South Korea) meet-ings held in Bangkok in July. Indonesia, a proponent of wider regional cooperation in East Asia, found itself in an ironic situation. Its foreign minister could not find the time to attend the first foreign ministers' meeting of the ASEAN+3 group because he had to attend a party con-gress at home. Nevertheless, ASEAN+3 members expressed their strong support for Indonesia's territorial integrity and unity.

Indonesia's role and involvement in the global arena have also been minimal. In May, Indonesia hosted a UN-sponsored conference on the illicit trafficking of small arms and light weapons. In July, Indonesia was appointed as the chair of the Colombo Plan Council, an organization whose primary aim is to promote closer economic and social coopera-tion among developing countries in Asia Pacific.

While Indonesia's active participation in regional and global affairs was not very significant, President Wahid continued his own form of international activism through extensive travel, seeking greater inter-national support for the country's ailing economy and fragile territorial integrity. However, the president's claims that Indonesia intended to play a meaningful role in helping to solve regional conflicts, such as that in the Philippine province of Mindanao, seemed mainly to be a matter of rhetoric with little follow-up. Similarly, Wahid's earlier foreign policy agenda of creating an "Asian coalition" involving Indonesia, China, and India, as well as Japan and Singapore, has not proceeded with any concrete steps and has invoked little interest among the other parties concerned.

Indonesia's continuing internal political and economic uncertainties are likely to place serious constraints on Indonesia's ability (and declared intention) to play a more active role in regional and global security affairs in 2001 and beyond.

9 Japan

THE SECURITY ENVIRONMENT

Japan began 2001 with the same sluggish economy and political confusion that characterized 2000 after a decade of economic decline. Positive developments such as corporate reforms, initiatives to advance information technology (IT), and a modicum of economic recovery did not improve Japan's outlook for the future, which continued to be clouded by a massive public debt, high levels of unemployment, and the rapid aging of the population. With deeply entrenched vested bureaucratic and political interests and a dearth of creative lawmakers, Japan's political leadership remained ineffectual, leading to growing apathy, frustration, and distrust of politics among the public. Externally, despite some activism on foreign and security policy, Japan's influence in the international arena was perceived by many observers to be declining.

INTERNAL   Throughout 2000, the political scene in Japan remained fluid. Following the breakup of negotiations with then Prime Minister Obuchi Keizō for a possible political realignment, the Liberal Party (LP) under Ozawa Ichirō left the coalition government led by the Liberal Democratic Party (LDP) in April 2000. This move split the LP and produced the New Conservative Party, which remained in the ruling coalition. In the same month, Prime Minister Obuchi's sudden stroke triggered a backstage deal by a handful of the LDP's old guard in which Mori Yoshirō was chosen as Obuchi's successor. The opaqueness of this succession process led to much public criticism.

In the general elections for the House of Representatives (Lower House) held in June, the LDP and its coalition partners (the New

Kōmeitō and the New Conservative Party) managed to secure a majority. Nevertheless, the results dealt a serious blow to the coalition government. The LDP won only 233 of the 480 seats, a substantial drop from its preelection strength of 267, while the opposition Democratic Party of Japan garnered 127 seats, up from 95.

With the economy still in the doldrums and public approval ratings for the Mori government dropping below 20 percent, Katō Kōichi, former secretary-general of the LDP, broke with Prime Minister Mori and called for his resignation in mid-November. Katō tried to mobilize support for an opposition-sponsored no-confidence motion against the Mori cabinet, but he backed down at the last minute when faced with threats of expulsion from the LDP.

One of the year's positive developments was Tokyo's realization that IT would be the key to prosperity in the 21st century, impacting the sluggish Japanese economy and leading to further globalization. The Mori government took the initiative to establish a "Japanese IT society," aimed at enabling every Japanese to enjoy the benefits of IT. Furthermore, at the July Group of Eight summit in Okinawa, Tokyo advocated international efforts to address the global digital divide.

In January 2000, both houses of the Diet created constitutional review panels to assess constitutional issues that were regarded as taboo during much of the postwar period. Although these panels have no authority to initiate constitutional revisions, they may open the way for a new interpretation or even an outright amendment of the constitution. The government's constitutional interpretation that sees Japan as prohibited from executing the right of collective self-defense is one of the most controversial issues. Proponents for a wider interpretation of the Constitution stress that the government's interpretation constrains greater Japanese participation in UN peacekeeping and alliance cooperation with the United States.

During 2000, the late Prime Minister Obuchi presented a report commissioned by him on Japan's goals in the 21st century. This report, titled *The Frontier Within: Individual Empowerment and Better Governance in the New Millennium,* provoked a heated debate over the nation's long-term objectives. It discerned five major trends that may critically influence Japan's future: globalization; global literacy, especially computer skills and English; the IT revolution; scientific advances, for example, in the life sciences and biotechnology; and falling birth rates and an aging population. The report made numerous far-reaching proposals, including directly electing the prime minister, forging *rinkō* (neighborly relations) with China and Korea, strengthening civil society and good governance, establishing an immigration policy, adopting English as an official second language, and defining Japan's world role as a global civilian power. Some analysts observed that the report generated an unprecedented debate over Japan's identity in the new century. Specifically, two conflicting visions of its future identity crystallized: Japan as an open, multilingual, and multiracial nation versus Japan as a homogenous, monolingual, and largely closed nation.

EXTERNAL   While Japan's alliance with the United States remains central, Japan's foreign and security policy witnessed a greater degree of activism in 2000 than in previous years. At the global level, Japan intensified its advocacy of UN reform. At the UN Millennium Summit in September, Prime Minister Mori urged early implementation of Security Council reforms. Foreign Minister Kōno Yōhei echoed this theme. He pressed Japan's case for a permanent UN Security Council seat, arguing that Japan was ready to play a larger role in promoting economic development, "human security," and disarmament and nonproliferation.

In the Asia Pacific region, Japan departed slightly from its preoccupation with the United States and sought to forge friendly ties with several countries of strategic importance. Both economic and strategic considerations motivated Prime Minister Mori's visit in August to Southwest Asia, including India and Pakistan. Tokyo's cultivation of ties with India reflected not only concerns about nuclear proliferation in South Asia but also Japan's strategic interest in balancing the rise of China's regional influence.

Japan also became increasingly eager to strengthen regional cooperation in East Asia. This was manifested in Tokyo's strong support for the ASEAN+3 (China, Japan, and South Korea) process; regularized China-Japan-South Korea summit meetings; the establishment of the Japan-ASEAN General Exchange Fund designed to provide assistance to new ASEAN (Association of Southeast Asian Nations) members, such as Vietnam and Cambodia; and the extension of US$80 billion in financial assistance to the region.

Japan's changing attitude toward regional security was also exhibited in its proposal for the creation of a regional maritime force to patrol the Strait of Malacca. In 1999, acts of actual or attempted piracy in Indonesian waters reportedly doubled to 113 incidents from 60 in 1998, and in the first three months of 2000 four Japanese tankers were subject to pirate attacks in the Strait of Malacca. As a result, Japan's

Maritime Safety Agency suggested in April that the Japanese Coast Guard, with more than 50 large offshore patrol vessels, could participate in a regional maritime force. China's reaction to this proposal was reportedly cautious, even though several ASEAN countries responded favorably.

Although Japan's overall relationship with China remained stable, relations were somewhat strained. China's increasing military expenditures, growing missile stockpiles, and expanding naval operations near Japan caused considerable concern. Japan's defense white paper reported that there had been 14 sightings of Chinese naval vessels within Japan's territorial waters in the first six months of 2000, 27 in 1999, and only two in 1998. China also intensified its marine research activities in Japan's Exclusive Economic Zones (EEZs) during 2000. These circumstances prodded Tokyo to postpone a planned US$161 million loan package to China and review Official Development Assistance (ODA) to China.

In August, Foreign Minister Kōno brought up these issues during his visit to China. Both sides agreed to set up an advance notification mechanism for China's maritime-research activities. Subsequently, Tokyo decided to extend the loan package to China. The Japanese public's feelings toward China were soothed when Chinese Premier Zhu Rongji, on his visit to Japan in October, appeared on television in a dialogue with ordinary Japanese citizens. During Zhu's visit, the two countries' governments also confirmed the opening of a hotline between them and agreed to strengthen their security dialogue and defense exchanges, including visits of naval vessels.

In the November 1997 Krasnoyarsk Agreement, Japan and Russia had agreed to do their "utmost" to conclude a peace treaty by the year 2000 and resolve their dispute over the Northern Territories. Although vigorous diplomatic efforts to achieve this goal followed, by the end of 2000 little actual progress had taken place. Nevertheless, during his visit to Japan in September, Russian President Vladimir Putin confirmed that Russia would abide by the 1956 Japan-Soviet Joint Declaration, which provided for the return of Habomai and Shikotan islands—two of the disputed territories—after the conclusion of a peace treaty. The Japan-Russia relationship was also strengthened by the signing of 15 agreements on bilateral cooperation. These included agreements on Japanese assistance for dismantling Russia's retired nuclear submarines, collaboration between Japan's Coast Guard and Russia's border patrol, and promotion of economic and scientific cooperation.

During 2000, Japan's relations with South Korea were strengthened due to reciprocal visits by top-level leaders and a wide range of cooperative measures. The two countries confirmed their agreement that North Korea's nuclear and missile development programs are of common concern to Japan, South Korea, and the United States.

Developments on the Korean peninsula in 2000 created new circumstances for Japan's relations with North Korea. In March, Tokyo announced that it would send 100,000 tons of rice to Pyongyang. In April, Tokyo and Pyongyang reopened negotiations on establishing diplomatic relations, which had been suspended since 1992. Subsequent developments on the Korean peninsula, especially the inter-Korean summit between Kim Dae Jung and Kim Jong Il in June and diplomatic reconciliation efforts by several Western countries, including the United States, spurred Tokyo to accelerate the normalization of relations with Pyongyang. In October, Tokyo decided to offer an additional 500,000 tons of rice to Pyongyang, far exceeding the 195,000 tons of food assistance requested by the UN World Food Program. However, two problematic issues continue to impede normalization: the alleged abductions of Japanese citizens by North Korean agents and Pyongyang's demand for an apology and compensation for Japan's colonial rule of the Korean peninsula.

DEFENSE POLICIES AND ISSUES

DEFENSE POLICIES   Article 9 of the Constitution continues to define the two main factors influencing Japan's defense policies: renunciation by Japan of the use or threat of force; and the Japan-U.S. alliance, which provides Japan's ultimate security guarantee. During 2000, Japan retained the main features of its basic defense policies, including an "exclusively defense-oriented policy," and the three nonnuclear principles of not possessing, producing, or permitting the introduction into Japan of nuclear weapons, while upgrading defense capabilities and strengthening Japan-U.S. security arrangements.

The functions and objectives of Japan's Self-Defense Forces (SDF) have been substantially expanded through the new National Defense Program Outline in 1995 and the revised Guidelines for U.S.-Japan Defense Cooperation in 1997. After the expiration of the Mid-term Defense Program (MTDP) in fiscal 2000, the Security Council approved on December 15, 2000, a new MTDP covering the period from 2001 through 2005, with a projected budget of ¥25.16 trillion (US$219 billion at US$1 = ¥114.75). The new five-year program includes the acquisition of four aerial tankers, two 13,500-ton-class helicopter-carrying warships, and two destroyers equipped with the Aegis system. It also calls for the establishment of a special unit within the Ground Self-Defense Force (GSDF) to deal with guerrilla attacks; improvements in the capacity to respond to natural disasters and attacks involving nuclear, biological, and chemical weapons; and strengthening information technology, command, and control systems within the SDF.

The Japan-U.S. security alliance remained firm in 2000. In September, Tokyo and Washington signed a five-year renewal of the Special Measures Agreement. This agreement requires Japan to pay for most of the labor, utilities, and relocation costs associated with hosting the forward deployment of U.S. forces in Japan. Moreover, to complement three laws enacted in 1999 to implement the Guidelines for U.S.-Japan Defense Cooperation, the Diet in November enacted a bill on ship inspection. This bill grants Japanese authorities the right to inspect suspicious foreign vessels on the high seas to enforce international economic sanctions.

DEFENSE BUDGET   Japan's defense budget for fiscal year 2000 was ¥4,935 billion (US$43.0 billion), an increase of 0.3 percent over 1999. The defense budget does not include spending on the Coast Guard or on pensions for armed forces personnel. The ratio of defense spending to gross national product was projected to be 0.989 percent in 2000. The defense budget included ¥14.0 billion (US$1.22 billion) for relocating several U.S. military facilities on Okinawa as outlined by the Japan-U.S. Special Action Committee on Okinawa (SACO). Of the 2000 defense budget, 44.8 percent was allocated to personnel and provisions, 18.6 percent to equipment and materials, 18.1 percent to operational maintenance (including education and training), 11.1 percent to support U.S. forces in Japan, 3.4 percent to base and facilities maintenance, and 2.4 percent to research and development. As of March 2000, the SDF had approximately 236,821 active duty personnel, of whom 148,557 were in the GSDF, 42,655 in the Maritime Self-Defense Force (MSDF), 44,207 in the Air Self-Defense Force (ASDF), and 1,402 in the Joint Staff Council.

PROCUREMENT   At the end of the year 2000, more than 98 percent of the procurement targets set out in the Mid-term Defense Program for

1996–2000 had been achieved. Major equipment that Japan procured or started to procure in fiscal 2000 included the following:

- For the GSDF, 18 Type-90 tanks, 30 armored vehicles, seven artillery 155-mm howitzer FH70s, nine multiple-launch rocket systems, three multipurpose helicopters (UH-60JA), two transport helicopters (CH-47JA), and four OH-1 helicopters.
- For the MSDF, one 4,600-ton-class destroyer, one 2,700-ton-class submarine, one 510-ton-class minesweeper, two 200-ton-class missile craft, and seven patrol helicopters (SH-60J).
- For the ASDF, nine fighter-support aircraft (F-2), two improved early-warning aircraft (E-2C), one transport helicopter (CH-47J), two rescue helicopters (UH-60J), two rescue and search aircraft (U-125A), and nine intermediate-level jet trainers (T-4).

OKINAWA   Although Okinawa Prefecture accounts for only 0.6 percent of Japan's total land area, three-fourths of the land area covered by U.S. bases in Japan is concentrated in the prefecture. In 1999, Okinawa Governor Inamine Keiichi suggested that the prefecture would accept a plan to relocate the U.S. Futenma Air Station within Okinawa, provided that the United States only use the facility for a limited period of 15 years. The United States rejected this 15-year limitation proposal. Despite these difficulties, the Japanese government remains committed to implement the SACO final report that seeks to reduce and consolidate U.S. bases on Okinawa. Tokyo will also continue to negotiate with Washington, while working closely with the Okinawa prefectural government and local municipalities through the Replacement Facility Council.

MISSILE DEFENSE   Japan has already procured and deployed a limited lower-tier missile defense system, operating Patriot PAC-1 and PAC-2 missiles, as well as Hawk anti-aircraft missile systems. Negotiations are also under way to procure PAC-3 technology, including upgrades to existing missiles and ground equipment, under a deal that would allow for PAC-3 production under license in Japan. In addition, the MSDF has deployed four Aegis-class destroyers that can be upgraded and integrated into a U.S. theater missile defense (TMD) system. Finally, Japan purchased several AWACS early-warning planes that can be used as sensors in a U.S. TMD system.

The defense budget for fiscal 2000 earmarked ¥2 billion (US$17.4 million) for funding the joint TMD research program with the United

States. This reflects Japan's continued commitment to develop jointly with the U.S. navy a TMD system to safeguard Japan against a possible ballistic missile threat. However, effective operation of such a system will require highly integrated command and control systems with the SDF and U.S. forces. Moreover, due to the requirement of considerable financial resources for TMD and its potential for harming relations with China, Japan may delay its decision on actual deployment of an upper-tier TMD system for the indefinite future.

Contributions to Regional and Global Security

GLOBAL AND REGIONAL   The Japan-U.S. alliance remains vitally important not only for Japan's security but for peace and stability in the Asia Pacific region. Against this backdrop, Japan keenly supports regional efforts such as the Asia-Pacific Economic Cooperation (APEC) forum, the ASEAN Regional Forum (ARF), and the Asia-Europe Meeting (ASEM). Tokyo also actively backs global institutions, including the United Nations, the World Trade Organization (WTO), and global arms control and nonproliferation regimes such as the Comprehensive Test Ban Treaty (CTBT) and the Nonproliferation Treaty (NPT).

In Northeast Asia, Japan during 2000 continued to strengthen its security dialogues and defense exchanges with neighboring countries, specifically China, Russia, and South Korea. The establishment in 1999 of the Trilateral Coordination and Oversight Group, an arrangement between Japan, South Korea, and the United States, was a significant step forward in buttressing mechanisms for consultation on North Korea.

ECONOMIC CONTRIBUTIONS   In 1999 for the ninth consecutive year, Tokyo managed to retain its position as the world's largest donor to developing countries, expending ¥1.745 trillion (US$15.24 billion). However, Japan's ratio of ODA to GNP was 0.35 percent, the seventh highest among the 22 major aid donors in the Organisation for Economic Co-operation and Development's (OECD's) Development Assistance Committee. Concerns about the country's financial problems prompted the government to review its ODA policy in 2000. In November, LDP Policy Research Council Chairman Kamei Shizuka proposed a drastic 30 percent reduction in ODA, triggering an intense debate within the government. Nonetheless, the fiscal 2001 ODA reduction is expected to be 3 percent or less compared with fiscal 2000's ODA level.

Japan's ODA policy guidelines for the five-year period from fiscal 1999 through fiscal 2003 call for promoting education, health care, and the empowerment of women in developing nations. However, in recent years political and strategic considerations have become prominent in Japan's foreign aid. In 2000, Tokyo reviewed its ODA to China, taking into account China's expanding military expenditures. Japan gave additional food aid to North Korea, and food and medical assistance to Yugoslavia. Finally, Tokyo decided to provide financial assistance to the UN Development Program to assist with the development of human resources in East Timor.

UN PEACEKEEPING   Japan's contribution to UN peacekeeping remains limited to logistical support assignments, such as transportation and construction services. The core functions of peacekeeping, including the monitoring of disarmament agreements and the patrolling of buffer zones, continue to be "frozen" pending new legislation. In 2000, Japan sustained its participation in the UN Disengagement Observer Force (UNDOF) in the Golan Heights and its involvement in the UN Transitional Administration in East Timor (UNTAET).

10 Republic of Korea

THE SECURITY ENVIRONMENT

The year 2000 marked a critical turning point for the Korean peninsula. The historical summit meeting between the leaders of the two Koreas in June opened the possibility of tremendous change taking place, not only regarding regional security but also concerning South Korea's domestic political landscape. Developments in inter-Korean relations during 2000 are even more significant when viewed against the situation just a year before. Although the overall security situation on the peninsula had stabilized by then, due to closer trilateral coordination among South Korea, Japan, and the United States in dealing with North Korea, nobody expected such dramatic changes in inter-Korean relations before Kim Dae Jung's visit to Pyongyang was announced in March 2000.

INTERNAL ISSUES   South Korea is considered a successful example of the East Asian model for economic development and political democratization. Since the inauguration of the country's first opposition leader, Kim Dae Jung, as president in 1998, the government has pursued political reform, economic restructuring, and diplomatic initiatives for dismantling the cold war structure on the Korean peninsula. However, as the Kim Dae Jung presidency approaches the middle of its five-year term, new troubles coupled with existing problems have emerged. Polarizing and vicious maneuvering continues to characterize the country's politics, jeopardizing policy stability and undermining the strength of the president. One result has been that President Kim's effective policies have not resulted in a rise in his popularity. Even President Kim's

Nobel Prize has failed to strengthen his hand against an increasingly vocal political opposition at home.

Political competition and rivalry became acute with the parliamentary elections in April 2000. Regional antagonisms, factional politics, and the authoritarian internal organization of parties negatively influenced the elections. Following the elections, a web of controversies beset the ruling camp, including the railroading of a legislative reform bill, a protracted dispute over the medical system, allegations that the ruling party attempted to influence a probe into campaign spending by parliamentary candidates, and suspicions that one of the president's closest confidants was involved in a bank loan scandal. Evidently, the government remained complacent with its success in overcoming the financial crisis of late 1997 and lax in carrying out necessary public and private sector reforms.

Financial and corporate reforms also began to slow, while public funds injected into ailing banks produced no tangible gains. In particular, key corporate and financial reforms floundered because the National Assembly failed to pass the relevant legislation. In addition, the stock market's nose dive, the surge of crude oil prices, and the fall in the price of computer chips, one of Korea's largest export items, threatened the country with economic hardship. Certainly, the economic situation in 2000 was not as serious as the economic crisis of 1997, since interest and foreign exchange rates remained stable and foreign exchange reserves were abundant. However, Korea entered 2001 with a looming fear of a second economic crisis as opinion polls indicated deepening public distrust of the legislature and the political community as a whole.

Ironically, President Kim and his administration have become entangled in deepening internal discord over the past three years, as the government has made significant progress in improving relations with North Korea and guiding the national economy out of the 1997 financial crisis. Extreme partisan confrontation, regionalism, and favoritism have characterized domestic politics throughout the Kim administration. In fact, President Kim is convinced that the opposition is using government scandals as a stage for a political offensive, while the opposition is convinced that the president is overlooking the gravity of the problems currently facing the nation. President Kim's administration, without effectively engaging political opponents and the public at home, will find it difficult to pursue economic reforms as well as external initiatives.

EXTERNAL SECURITY   *Inter-Korean Summit.* Emerging from decades of self-imposed isolation, North Korea began to engage in diplomatic initiatives to improve relations with foreign countries, gain global assistance, and join international organizations. However, until early spring 2000, North Korea had shown little interest in holding talks with South Korea. Conventional wisdom held that improvements in North Korea–U.S. relations and the normalization of North Korea–Japan relations were needed before North-South relations could significantly improve. These assumptions changed as President Kim Dae Jung proposed in March 2000 a resumption of the government-to-government inter-Korean dialogue. Kim's initiative included Seoul's commitment to assist Pyongyang in rebuilding its ailing economy by providing loans to the North. To alleviate financial hardship, Pyongyang had by 1999 admitted about 180,000 South Korean tourists to Mt. Kumgang, allowed more than 100 southern businesses to set up operations, and increased trade with the South to US$330 million.

Despite these developments, the summit announcement came as a complete surprise. The North's willingness signaled a new sense of confidence that it could maintain its regime internally even while reaching out for help. Six years after the death of Kim Il Sung, Kim Jong Il seems convinced that he has consolidated his own position and built a political system capable of withstanding external influences. Thus, North Korea decided to look to the South for support, a move it presumably saw as providing increased leverage vis-à-vis the United States.

To implement the summit's joint declaration, South Korea launched later in 2000 a railroad project to open the first direct transportation link between the two Koreas. Additionally, 200,000 tons of fertilizer and 600,000 tons of food aid provided in the form of long-term food loans were donated to the North. In return, South Korea sought to conclude agreements on avoidance of double taxation and investment guarantees for South Korean businesses investing in the North. The South also expressed a keen interest in implementing military confidence-building measures, such as giving prior notice on troop movements and exercises, opening a North-South military hot line, and arranging regular meetings between military and defense officials. However, the two Koreas have made little overall progress on security matters affecting the Korean peninsula. The North seems to be taking a two-track approach. Pyongyang primarily talks to Washington about security matters and seeks economic assistance from the South.

Ultimately, the summit has allowed both Koreas to make major strides in improving inter-Korean relations by opening a line of communication between the two leaders and creating at least an appearance of harmonious relations. Whatever the exact mix of motivations, the summit is having a positive effect on the domestic and/or international political standing of the two leaders. Despite his domestic problems, President Kim Dae Jung received great international praise and won the Nobel Peace Prize for his contribution to peace on the Korean peninsula. It is premature, however, to conclude that the summit has built substantial mutual confidence or that an era of cooperation has arrived between the two Koreas. In the South, the domestic political and economic situation will likely become increasingly important in determining the sustainability of Kim's "Sunshine Policy."

In South Korea, the opposition party has repeatedly criticized the government for giving Pyongyang too much and receiving too little in return. The opposition has also voiced its suspicion that North Korea's leadership is trying to manipulate South Korean politics, pointing out that heightened expectations from the summit have served to lower the public's guard against the undiminished military threat from the North. Clearly, it remains to be seen whether North Korea's policy reflects a fundamental change or just a temporary tactical shift. It seems inevitable that North Korea will open up and change to some degree, but that its leadership will attempt to closely control this process. Indeed, signs of this phenomenon have already appeared. Kim Jong Il has tried to limit exchanges between the two Koreas to the economic area, while allowing people-to-people exchanges such as family reunions only to the extent necessary to sustain improved relations with the South. The question for the South is how much it should offer and how much it should demand in return.

South Korea–U.S. Relations. The thawing of relations on the Korean peninsula has generated hope that North Korea is ready to join the rest of the world as a constructive player. However, with inter-Korean rapprochement, anti-American sentiment has reemerged among some South Koreans. For this group, North Korea is seen more positively, perhaps even as a partner in unification, while the United States is regarded as a stumbling block to unification and an arrogant superpower. Anti-American sentiment in South Korea is also due to a number of unresolved issues in South Korea–U.S. relations. These include the alleged massacre of South Korean refugees by American troops at No Gun Ri during the Korean War, disturbance and damage caused by bombing accidents at the U.S. air force firing range in Maehyang-ri, and the release of toxic chemicals into the Han River from the U.S. army base in Seoul. Renegotiating the U.S. Status of Forces Agreement (SOFA) is another thorny issue, since the majority of Koreans feel that the SOFA has not been addressed earnestly by the United States. Thus, North-South rapprochement has provided a convenient platform for opponents of the U.S. troop presence in South Korea to promote their cause before the South Korean public.

With continuing rapprochement and anti-American sentiment, the South Korea–U.S. alliance is likely to undergo significant change, perhaps even involving a modification in the status of U.S. forces in Korea. Nonetheless, a strong alliance with the United States remains the key to South Korea's national security, economic prosperity, and the continuation of improved relations with North Korea. The South Korean and U.S. governments face the challenge of keeping the alliance intact. This requires stronger cognizance by the South Korean public of the importance of the South Korea–U.S. relationship, and added U.S. sensitivity toward a more self-confident and assertive South Korea. Clearly, the new U.S. administration faces the dual task of engaging its old enemy and maintaining good relations with its old friend on the Korean peninsula.

North Korea–U.S. Relations. Inter-Korean rapprochement was followed by an acceleration of North Korea–Japan normalization talks and a rapid improvement in North Korea–U.S. relations. This indicates North Korea's continuing diplomatic focus on the United States. Pyongyang seems to regard diplomatic recognition by Washington as a means to ensure regime survival. In October 2000, Kim Jong Il dispatched as his special envoy Jo Myong-rok, vice-marshal of the North Korean military and Kim's right-hand man, to Washington. In the historic North Korea–U.S. Joint Communiqué, the two sides agreed that improved relations are needed to ensure peace between North and South Korea and in the Asia Pacific region.

The communiqué also surprised many observers by hinting at a possible visit by U.S. President Bill Clinton to North Korea before the end of his term in January 2001. President Kim Dae Jung officially welcomed North Korea–U.S. rapprochement and encouraged President Clinton to visit Pyongyang. However, opinion leaders in Washington were more skeptical, fearing that the United States, without a verifiable agreement on the missile issue, would be overly generous to the North. As a result, the Clinton visit did not materialize.

Later in October, closely following Jo's visit to Washington, U.S.

Secretary of State Madeleine Albright visited Pyongyang. Representatives from the two countries discussed in detail ways to fashion a package deal that would restrain North Korea's long-range Taepodong missile program. One option discussed was the establishment of a consortium that would finance and launch a small North Korean commercial satellite. However, such a deal would fail to address important issues, specifically the North's shorter-range Nodong missiles that pose a direct threat to South Korea as well as Japan. North Korea appeared to be attempting to seal a deal with the Clinton administration, thus presenting a *fait accompli* to the new U.S. administration; however, at year's end no agreement had been finalized, and the next steps in U.S. policy on the Korean peninsula were left to the George W. Bush administration.

DEFENSE POLICIES AND ISSUES

Of South Korea's total 100 trillion won (US$79.11 billion at US$1 = 1,264 won) budget for fiscal year 2001, the defense budget is set at 15.4 trillion won (US$12.2 billion), up 6.5 percent from 2000. The government also plans to spend another 500 billion won (US$395.6 million) on economic cooperation with North Korea, compared to 100 billion won (US$79.11 million) earmarked in 2000. The Defense Ministry has allocated 5.3 trillion won (US$4.2 billion) to force-improvement programs, accounting for around 37 percent of the total defense budget. These programs include improving the military's strike force capability, specifically the deployment of 110 Israeli-made Harp missiles capable of striking anti-air missiles. The ministry has also set aside 230 billion won (US$182 million) to invest in the acquisition of strategic intelligence and battlefield surveillance equipment. Investment for future-oriented core arms procurement projects was increased by 9.4 percent, while research and development saw a 0.3 percent rise. Due to the weight given to these new projects, critical areas like ammunition and maintenance have been cut by 9.7 percent, to some degree compromising operational capability and undermining the defense industry.

South Korea also plans to spend 34.6 trillion won (US$27.3 billion) over the next five years on a new omnidirectional defense plan. This includes the construction of a 7,000-ton, KDX-3 Aegis-class destroyer and the introduction of AWACS and mid-air refueling tankers to the Republic of Korea AirForce in 2002 and 2005, respectively. This new strategy reflects a perceived need to be able to respond to threats from any direction, not just from North Korea. The advent of North-South reconciliation and the possibility of a future reduction in the U.S. troop presence in South Korea has prodded the Ministry of National Defense to consider how to marshal the resources necessary to compensate for a reduction in U.S. forces. Building on its long-term defense policy and efforts to create a future-oriented, high-tech military, the ministry will likely increase the size of the navy and air force and reduce the number of troops in the army while promoting an elite corps of soldiers. The army currently accounts for some 81 percent of South Korea's armed forces personnel.

CONTRIBUTIONS TO REGIONAL SECURITY

REGIONAL   Despite its own demanding security situation, South Korea has recently become actively involved in wider international affairs. At the UN Millennium Summit in September 2000, South Korea received global attention for the success of the inter-Korean summit, which enlisted international security support to aid the progress of inter-Korean relations. As part of its contribution to international peacekeeping operations, Seoul also dispatched 417 troops and additional personnel to the United Nations Transitional Administration in East Timor (UNTAET). With South Korea likely to assume the chairmanship of the United Nations General Assembly in 2001, Seoul sees it as imperative to make a visible contribution to world peace and stability.

In the wake of the inter-Korean summit, South Korea strongly urged the ASEAN Regional Forum (ARF) member countries to accept North Korea as a member. North Korea joined the security dialogue in July 2000 as the group's 23rd member. At a minimum, by joining the ARF, North Korea will need to assume a number of new responsibilities, such as presenting a yearly report on its security policy.

In October 2000, Seoul also hosted the Asia-Europe Meeting (ASEM), which adopted a comprehensive Asia-Europe Cooperation Framework (AECF) as the guiding principle for the future of the ASEM process. The AECF designates democracy, human rights, and the rule of law as the common vision of the multilateral body. Notably, the ASEM also approved Korea's proposal to establish a Trans-Eurasia network, and strongly supported the inter-Korean summit and the Korean Peninsula Energy Development Organization (KEDO) project.

NORTHEAST ASIA   South Korea has mapped out a new plan to establish a permanent peace mechanism on the Korean peninsula. This mechanism calls for North and South Korea to first reach agreement and subsequently for China and the United States to endorse it. Specifically, the mechanism tries to address the limited progress made after six rounds of Four-Party Talks. So far the Four-Party Talks have largely taken place in a two-in-four format with only North Korea and the United States discussing key issues. South Korea anticipates a reactivation of these talks, chiefly because the North Korea–U.S. Joint Communiqué stated that the Four-Party Talks are one available avenue to reduce tensions on the peninsula and bring an official end to the Korean War.

Currently, China, Japan, Russia, and the United States are reassessing their positions vis-à-vis the Korean peninsula. In the short to medium term, China has the most to gain diplomatically from radically improved relations between North and South Korea. As the visit by Kim Jong Il to China only a few days before the Korean summit underscored, China is back on center stage in Korean affairs. Kim Jong Il apparently visited China to secure some form of insurance in case the North's system is jeopardized as it opens up to the outside world. Russia and Japan are also interested in having a voice in Korean matters.

Clearly, chances for achieving a multilateral dialogue and peace mechanism for the Korean peninsula have increased. The Trilateral Coordination and Oversight Group (TCOG) among South Korea, Japan, and the United States was an example of efficient minilateral cooperation in dealing with North Korea, despite some grumbling among the members. Indeed, the international politics of the Korean peninsula are changing rapidly, with each country trying to secure a place for itself in determining the future of the two Koreas.

11 Malaysia

THE SECURITY ENVIRONMENT

Compared to Malaysia's security environment in the late 1990s, when the country was engulfed by the Asian financial crisis, recent months have seen a dramatic, positive turnaround. Despite these improvements, however, the country's overall domestic stability remains susceptible to renewed threats and challenges.

INTERNAL ENVIRONMENT *Economic Recovery*. Beginning in the second half of 1999, Malaysia's economy rebounded strongly from the retrenchment experienced during 1998 and early 1999 as a result of the Asian financial crisis. Expansionary fiscal policy, as well as the introduction of selective capital controls and the pegging of the Malaysian ringgit to the U.S. dollar, contributed. Gross domestic product declined in 1998 by 7.8 percent, but the rate of growth recovered to 5.8 percent in 1999, an estimated 7.5 percent in 2000, and a projected 7 percent in 2001. Malaysia's foreign reserves grew to US$32.3 billion in mid-October 2000, up from US$30.9 billion in 1999. The unemployment rate dropped from a high of 4.9 percent in 1998 to 3 percent in 1999 and 2.9 percent in 2000, which is considered full employment.

The government is continuing to pursue structural economic reforms. In July 1999, the restructuring of the financial sector was initiated with the aim of consolidating the country's 58 financial institutions into ten core banking groups. The 58 financial institutions include 21 commercial banks, 25 finance companies, and 12 merchant banks. However, progress in structural economic reform has been sluggish. Specifically, financial sector restructuring remains incomplete, corporate governance reforms have been slow, and corporations still lack working capital due to the continuing credit crunch. As in the rest of Southeast Asia, foreign direct investment inflows are weak and labor productivity is low. Because the Malaysian ringgit is pegged to the U.S. dollar, the appreciation of the U.S. dollar against regional currencies has reduced Malaysian competitiveness. Regional economic recovery, another important factor for Malaysia's domestic economy, is regarded as fragile, and growth prospects for 2001 in the major industrial countries, especially the United States and Japan, remain uncertain.

Political Environment. The country's recovery from the economic crisis helped defuse the political tensions that had threatened domestic stability from late 1998 into 2000. In September 1998, political tensions came to a head when Prime Minister Mahathir bin Mohammed dismissed his deputy prime minister and finance minister, Anwar Ibrahim. Subsequently, Anwar was charged and convicted of five charges of corruption in April 1999 and five charges of sodomy in August 2000, carrying a total sentence of 15 years (six years for corruption and nine years for sodomy). Anwar's sentences, regarded by many as too severe, did not elicit the kind of mass protest seen in 1998 at the time of his arrest. The convictions did, however, aggravate the simmering division among the country's Malay population, challenging Mahathir's political leadership from not only outside the United Malays National Organization (UMNO) but also within.

This division was clearly reflected in the November 1999 general election. While UMNO kept its two-thirds parliamentary majority, its share of the popular vote slid from 65 percent (in the 1995 election) to 56 percent. Consequently, UMNO lost 22 parliamentary seats, garnering only 72 seats out of 94. UMNO also ceded control of a second state assembly, Terengganu, allowing the opposition party—Parti Islam SeMalaysia (PAS, or the Islamic Party of Malaysia)—to control two out of Malaysia's 13 states. Perhaps most importantly, reports indicated that at least half of the country's ethnic Malays, the dominant political group, voted for the opposition.

As a result of UMNO's poor showing in the 1999 election, UMNO members called for party reforms at its 54th General Assembly in May 2000. Former deputy minister and head of the newly formed Human Rights Commission, Musa Hitam, expressed these demands, saying in an interview with a regional magazine that UMNO suffered from various ailments, including "support and agree syndrome," money politics, alienation from the grass roots, and a serious erosion of Malay support. Prime Minister Mahathir called on party members to be more responsive to the grass roots, especially the youth.

Even the top echelon of the party realized in 2000 that there was disaffection within the party and that Malay voters had to be won back. Since the May General Assembly, UMNO's leadership has become increasingly concerned that younger Malays, particularly university students, are supporting PAS. Following the General Assembly, UMNO tried to improve its image by introducing more independent-minded members to its Supreme Council. UMNO also moved to include more women, forming the Puteri UMNO, the female counterpart of the UMNO Youth Council, and appointing several female members to high government positions.

Despite external and internal criticism of UMNO, the country's political climate remains generally favorable to Mahathir's leadership. The Anwar saga has been almost completely relegated to the past, and the economy has returned to precrisis growth levels. However, UMNO and Mahathir face several future challenges. Anwar's supporters have intensified their campaign overseas, which could complicate Malaysia's external relations, particularly with the United States and some regional countries. UMNO also needs to regain the support of the majority of Malays. In 2004, when the next general elections will be held, 1.5 million new voters will be eligible, at least 60 percent of whom will be young Malays who are perceived to have little or no built-in loyalty to UMNO.

Other Concerns. In early July 2000, 15 members of Al Ma'unah (Brotherhood of Inner Power), officially described as an unknown Islamic cult, masqueraded as soldiers and broke into an army battalion camp in the northern state of Perak. The 15 men took four hostages, firearms, and ammunitions. Acting quickly, the military stormed the camp, captured the men, and recovered all arms and ammunitions that had been stolen. However, two hostages died in the skirmish. While official reports indicated that the activities of Al Ma'unah were effectively thwarted, the event came as a big shock to the country, alerting Malaysia's military to step up security at its military bases.

EXTERNAL ENVIRONMENT *Regional.* During 2000, Malaysia experienced the spillover effects of security problems in the Philippines. The Abu Sayaf Group (ASG), an insurgent group in the southern Philippines, abducted 21 hostages from the Malaysian resort of Sipadan in April. In September, the ASG abducted three more hostages from

Malaysia's Pandanan Islands. The hostages in the first kidnapping included three Malaysians, along with foreign tourists who were spending their holidays in Malaysia. In the second kidnapping case all three hostages were Malaysian. All but one of the hostages were later freed.

The Philippine government's handling of these events impacted Malaysia's security. Initially, long negotiations and large ransom payments did not produce hostage releases. Frustrated with this delay, the Philippine military bombarded parts of the Sulu Islands where the ASG was holed up. This caused an influx of so-called war refugees, unofficially estimated at about 50,000, into Malaysia from the Philippines. These incidents reminded Malaysia of how porous its borders are. As a result of the kidnappings and refugee influx, the Malaysian government deployed 600 additional personnel to aid the 170 men already assigned to patrol Malaysia's 170 offshore islands.

Malaysia also remains concerned about potential threats from Indonesia's political and economic crisis. Specifically, Malaysia fears that a further loss of central government control in Indonesia might trigger greater sectarian violence and secessionist movements, perhaps even Indonesia's fragmentation. Malaysia is already the largest host country for Indonesian immigrant workers, officially some 530,219 as of 1999. As the crisis in Indonesia continues, Malaysia expects more inflows of illegal Indonesian migrants. This threat has further accelerated Malaysia's efforts to protect the country's land and maritime borders.

The increase of piracy incidents in the Strait of Malacca in 1999–2000 has prompted Malaysia to conduct round-the-clock patrols with Indonesia and Singapore. Although Malaysia has welcomed Japan's offer to share communication technology and to exchange information, it has rejected the Japanese proposal to conduct joint patrols with Southeast Asian countries. Malaysia feels that the piracy problem can best be handled by seeking closer cooperation with its immediate neighbors.

Malaysia's relations with nearby Singapore have dramatically improved. In 1998–1999, several contentious issues strained bilateral relations. These included Singapore's demand that Malaysia move its customs, immigration, and quarantine facilities from downtown Singapore to the border; Singapore's refusal to allow Malaysians to withdraw their savings from Singapore's Central Provident Fund; negative comments about some former Malaysian leaders contained in the memoirs of Singapore's Senior Minister Lee Kuan Yew; and disputes over water sales to Singapore and over the Singapore Air Force's flight paths. While both governments have tried to resolve these issues quietly over past years, the most significant breakthrough occurred in August 2000 when Lee visited Malaysia for the first time in ten years. Lee's four-day visit led directly to discussions of outstanding issues between Prime Minister Mahathir and his Singaporean counterpart Goh Chok Tong.

Relations with Major Powers. Although Malaysia's relations with the United States had been strained by then U.S. Vice-President Al Gore's comments in Kuala Lumpur in 1998 supporting Malaysia's *reformasi* (reform) movement, Gore's remarks had no serious lasting effects on bilateral relations. Trade and investment relations between the two countries have been improving and the United States continues to be Malaysia's biggest export market. However, the Malaysian government strongly opposes proposed U.S. theater missile defense (TMD) and national missile defense (NMD) programs, an issue that will have to be dealt with by the new U.S. administration.

Malaysia has also continued to emphasize improving relations with China. Malaysia sees China's role in the region as important, especially China's support for the ASEAN+3 (China, Japan, and South Korea) summit—without which the sustained success of this regional enterprise cannot be assured. Prime Minister Mahathir takes, of course, a special interest in East Asian regionalism.

DEFENSE POLICIES AND ISSUES

DEFENSE STRATEGY   Malaysia's defense policy is currently under review with results expected in 2001. Fundamentally, Malaysia's defense policy is based on two premises: national resilience and conventional deterrence. Defense Minister Najib Tun Razak recently explained Malaysia's national security policy in a speech in September 2000 entitled "Toward a Comprehensive National Security Strategy." According to the minister, Malaysia's defense approach is multifaceted and multilayered; he likened the approach to concentric circles encompassing the global, regional, and national levels.

Malaysia considers itself weak at the global level. Nonetheless, Malaysia maintains a pragmatic approach toward powerful countries, including participating in military exercises. At the regional level, Malaysia works to ensure that regional issues do not pose a direct threat to its national security through strengthening ties with close neighbors. These ties have stabilized sufficiently so that when Singapore announced the purchase of 100 AIM-120C advanced medium-range guided missiles from the United States, Malaysia's defense minister stated his conviction that Singapore would not attack Malaysia.

Finally, at the national level, Malaysia regards national security as including a stable political system, a robust economy, a resilient society, and a strong military. Malaysia's military is now well positioned to deal with new threats. For example, due to the incursions and kidnappings experienced in 2000, the country's defense policy has shifted toward protecting maritime and land boundaries. The military will have a more direct role to play in protecting borders, a domain traditionally covered by the police. The military will also be expected to be directly involved in low intensity conflicts such as the Al Ma'unah arms heist.

SPENDING AND PROCUREMENT   Malaysia's defense forces are undergoing significant structural change. Emphasis is being placed on personnel training and advanced equipment acquisitions.

Malaysia's defense expenditures have increased from US$1.58 billion in 2000 to US$1.92 billion in 2001, representing 3.8 percent of the country's GDP. Priority is given to procurement programs that were canceled or postponed due to budget reductions in 1998. As announced by the defense minister, upgrading military firepower is a priority. The ministry plans to acquire 22 155-mm howitzer guns from South Africa and is considering the purchase of light helicopters for wider army reconnaissance operations. The army also placed orders to buy 211 tanks from Turkey, with the first batch to be delivered in 2001. Malaysia's Defense Technologies Sdn. Bhd., a member of the DRB-Hicom group, is preparing to locally assemble some of the tanks.

The Defense Ministry has also ordered Super Lynx helicopters for the Malaysian navy and is considering the purchase of guided missiles for the Super Lynx helicopters to give them longer distance firepower. Finally, Malaysia has announced plans to buy at least one submarine as part of its plan to build a new naval base at Teluk Sepanggar Bay, Sabah State, on Borneo, East Malaysia.

CONTRIBUTIONS TO REGIONAL AND GLOBAL SECURITY

Malaysia continues to be active in strengthening regional and global security. At the regional level, Malaysia remains committed to the Association of Southeast Asian Nations (ASEAN) and the ASEAN Regional

Forum (ARF). Malaysia participated in the ARF Senior Officials Development Program held in Brunei Darussalam during April 2000. Within ASEAN, Malaysia's diplomat Dato Ismail Razali has been chosen as the UN Special Envoy to carry out the United Nation's mission in Myanmar. This mission is attempting to explore efforts at national reconciliation in Myanmar. While this mission falls within the ambit of the United Nations, the support of core ASEAN countries is crucial because Myanmar is an ASEAN member. Malaysia's role in this mission is thus highly significant.

Malaysia has also been active in the establishment and progress of the ASEAN+3 grouping. The first informal summit of ASEAN+3 was held in Kuala Lumpur in 1997 at the height of the Asian financial crisis. The ideas and initiatives of the grouping, particularly to deepen and widen economic cooperation, reflect Malaysia's vision of an East Asia Economic Grouping announced as early as 1990. After the Asian financial crisis, Malaysia has especially promoted the establishment of an Asian Monetary Fund within the context of the ASEAN+3.

Malaysia also participates in the Organization of the Islamic Conference (OIC). The 27th Session of the Islamic Conference of Foreign Ministers was held in Kuala Lumpur in June 2000. At that meeting, Malaysia was included as the seventh member of the committee appointed by the OIC to oversee the implementation of the peace accord between the Moro National Liberation Front (MNLF) and the Philippine government.

Finally, Malaysia was heavily involved in the Group of 77's South Summit held in Havana, Cuba, in April 2000. Malaysia proposed that the G77 should present its views to the G7 governments at their scheduled meeting in July. In Havana, G77 member countries also agreed on the objective of speaking with one voice at the World Trade Organization (WTO).

12 Mongolia

THE SECURITY ENVIRONMENT

Geographically, Mongolia is the largest land-locked state between Russia and China. It occupies an important geo-strategic position on the Asian continent, at the crossroads of the political, economic, and cultural interests of the region's great powers and the junction of the world's major religions. Its large territory contrasts with a relatively small population of 2.6 million. These factors together define Mongolia's security problem and affect its security outlook.

INTERNAL   Since early 1990, Mongolia has experienced rapid transformation. The oldest communist state of Asia became the first Asian country to abandon one-party communist rule and make the transition to a democratic and market economy system. The most outstanding aspect of Mongolia's transformation was political reform. Supported by a broad-based consensus, this reform program unfolded smoothly, swiftly, and thoroughly. Mongolia developed a multiparty parliamentary system. In 2000, there were 12 registered political parties, four of which held seats in the State Great Hural (Parliament). In Mongolia's political system, the prime minister is nominated by the president and approved by Parliament. The armed forces are under civilian control and the minister and deputy minister of defense are civilians.

Among the countries that moved from centrally planned to market economy systems during the past decade, Mongolia stands out as making one of the most rapid transitions. Macroeconomic stabilization measures, the privatization of state assets, and public sector and legal reforms were pursued to give the private sector the best chance of success

in a competitive global economy. The program of economic stabilization and structural reform pursued since 1991 has had two main components. First, Mongolia liberalized prices, factor markets, and foreign
trade. In fact, Mongolia was for several years one of the few countries
in the world where tariffs and duties on imports were largely abolished.
Tariffs have since been reintroduced for revenue purposes at a level of
5 percent. Exports are exempt from taxation.

Second, Mongolia undertook a comprehensive privatization program during the early 1990s. Livestock, the main sector of the Mongolian economy, was completely privatized, as was almost 100 percent
of the country's housing sector. This program dramatically decreased
the government's involvement in economic affairs and boosted private
initiative. Currently, the private sector produces more than 60 percent
of Mongolia's gross domestic product.

Due to strict monetary policy, Mongolia curbed inflation, limiting
increases in the consumer price index to 10 percent per year by the end
of 1999. In addition, economic growth gained momentum, sustained
mainly by the trade, service, agriculture, and mining sectors. In 1999,
Mongolia recorded 3.5 percent real growth in GDP and an unemployment rate of 6 percent.

With economic and political reforms, new and numerous freedoms
have emerged in modern Mongolia. Mongolians now have the right to
own property and run a business. The country has achieved flourishing
arts, an open media, and freedom of expression and movement. However, as in other transition countries, Mongolia's reform process has not
been without difficulties. The sudden withdrawal of massive subsidies
provided by the former Soviet Union, the country's landlocked geogra-
phy, and its underdeveloped infrastructure have handicapped the transition to a market economy and created adverse effects for the populace.

The most serious threat to Mongolia's future concerns economic
security, which is the cornerstone of the country's independence and sovereignty. Therefore, the Mongolian government has concentrated its
efforts on macroeconomic stabilization, private sector development,
financial sector reform, and the promotion of export-oriented industries. Nonetheless, there are several economic matters of concern, including the sectoral composition of economic growth, the economy's
capacity to generate employment and income, regional aspects of development, and especially Mongolia's economic dependence on neighboring powers, particularly China. Mongolian producers worry about
the increasing prevalence of Chinese capital in the domestic market.

For example, China's huge cashmere manufacturers have bought up Mongolian wool at high prices, thus undermining Mongolia's own cashmere-processing industry. The Mongolian government believes that it must balance China's economic power by attracting higher levels of foreign assistance and investment from the West, Japan, and South Korea.

EXTERNAL   Mongolia's external security is to a large extent defined by Mongolia's relations with its neighbors, Russia and China. Mongolia's geographical location between the two great powers has been historically a major, and in many cases the decisive, factor in shaping the country's destiny. Consequently, the normalization of relations between Russia and China has greatly improved Mongolia's immediate security environment. In the absence of territorial disputes, no imminent external threat is perceived by Mongolia.

In the early 1990s, Mongolian policymakers debated heatedly on how to structure the country's relations with its powerful neighbors. Should Mongolia maintain an alliance or special relationship with Russia, bearing in mind Mongolia's history and economic dependence on Russia? Should Mongolia declare strict neutrality, like Switzerland? Or should Mongolia find another suitable "prescription," taking into account the country's geopolitical realities and the interests of its neighbors?

In the debate, the first option was rejected due to recent experience. During the Sino-Soviet "cold war" between 1960 and the mid-1980s, Soviet troops were stationed in Mongolia, raising the specter of the two "red giants" using Mongolia as a battlefield. The second option was also rejected on the grounds that strict neutrality is very difficult to sustain for a small, economically weak, landlocked state. Strict neutrality would require a degree of political and economic weight that Mongolia does not possess.

Finally, political realism and pragmatism prodded the Mongolian government to adopt a foreign policy concept that emphasizes the use of political and diplomatic means to ensure Mongolia's security interests. This foreign policy is based on an open, multilateral approach designed to overcome Mongolia's former isolation from the outside world, to accelerate the country's development, and to give the country more political and economic weight. Most importantly, Mongolia's foreign policy concept seeks to create credible counterweights to China and Russia by fostering close relations with "third neighbors." These third neighbors—countries that have consistently supported Mongolia's democratization, such as the United States, Japan, and other industrialized countries—are intended to play a stabilizing role in Mongolia's relations with its contiguous neighbors. Nonetheless, Mongolia's foreign policy also focuses on directly balancing the power of both Russia and China by strengthening trust and mutually beneficial cooperation with each of them.

Mongolia and the Russian Federation. In order to achieve balance in its relations with neighboring countries, Mongolia has been seeking to invigorate relations with Russia. Some tentative steps were taken during the 1990s, such as the signing of the Treaty on Friendly Relations and Cooperation in 1993, but little overall progress was made, especially compared to Mongolia's improving relations with China, Japan, and the United States. In part, this was due to the fact that until recently Russia had little interest in closer ties with Mongolia.

President Vladimir Putin's visit to Mongolia in November 2000, the first top-level visit by a Russian/Soviet leader in 26 years, may have marked the start of a long-awaited improvement in relations. At the end of Putin's visit, the 25-point Ulaanbaatar Declaration was issued, which outlined a framework for the future course of Mongolia-Russia relations. The main emphasis was on future economic cooperation between the two countries. However, attention was also given to defense cooperation, specifically military-to-military exchanges, the training of Mongolian servicemen, and issues related to the repair and technical servicing of Russian military equipment used by the Mongolian Armed Forces.

These arrangements are only beginning to be implemented. The renewal of Mongolia-Russia relations by no means implies a resumption of Mongolia's previous "satellite" relationship with Russia. However, Mongolia hopes for a speedy resumption of defense cooperation with Russia to amend the current imbalance in Mongolia's relations with its two closest neighbors.

Mongolia and China. Diplomatic relations between the People's Republic of China (PRC) and Mongolia were established in October 1949. From 1949 to 1962, the bilateral relationship developed rapidly. Then China-Mongolia relations stalled from the 1960s until the mid-1980s. Since 1989, however, they have revived. In particular, with the signing of the Agreement on Friendly Relations and Cooperation in 1994, cooperation between the two countries has expanded rapidly.

During the 1990s, Mongolia and China resolved all border issues and set up ten border passage points to foster interactions between these areas. As a result, frontier trade increased rapidly, leading to a substantial increase in the overall volume of trade between Mongolia and China. By 2000, China had become Mongolia's second largest trading partner. Generally, Mongolia exports raw materials of animal origin to China and imports commodity products from its southern neighbor. Beginning in 1990, Mongolia and China also reestablished defense cooperation, including mutual visits by high-level military officials, competitions among military sports teams and athletes, language training for Mongolian servicemen in China, and humanitarian aid from the Chinese Ministry of Defense to the Mongolian Ministry of Defense.

On the political front, Mongolia and China frequently exchange high-level delegations. Although there are no major unresolved issues between the two countries, several sensitive trouble spots remain. First, while Mongolia considers Taiwan as an inseparable part of the PRC, Mongolia reserves the right to develop economic and civilian relations with Taiwan. Second, Mongolian Buddhist devotees are inclined to invite the Dalai Lama, the head of Lamaist Buddhism, to Mongolia, producing tensions with China. Finally, Mongolians are concerned about the large influx of Chinese legal and illegal capital dominating the domestic market. Mongolians also fear that increasing food imports from China might create food security problems in the future.

DEFENSE POLICIES AND ISSUES

Beginning in the early 1990s, three developments have redefined Mongolia's defense policy. First, with the collapse of the Soviet Union the common defense system of the former Soviet bloc crumbled. This led to a cessation of outside military assistance for Mongolia. Drastic cuts in military expenditure occurred, and the reduction of the number of armed forces personnel and their military service terms followed, laying the foundation for later reforms. Second, the end of the cold war reduced tensions in the Asia Pacific region, especially in Mongolia's relations with Russia and China. Finally, far-reaching domestic political and social reforms encouraged the redefinition of Mongolia's defense policy.

The essence of Mongolia's current defense policy is to guarantee the country's independence, sovereignty, and territorial integrity. Defense activities are directed toward guarding Mongolia's state frontiers and defending the population against natural disasters and weapons of mass destruction. Mongolia's defense policy is based on the country's foreign policy concept and the "Basis of the State Military Policy," the fundamental legal document adopted by Parliament in 1998 to define Mongolia's defense policy.

According to this policy document, Mongolia's defense policy derives from the self-defense principles of the Constitution of Mongolia. The policy declares that Mongolia shall develop a compact and professional military suited to peacetime defense needs. The new defense policy also sets specific objectives, such as strengthening and upgrading Mongolia's armed forces into an integrated defense system; fostering confidence-building measures that encourage international cooperation; establishing an efficient defense budget; and strengthening civil-military relations. It also emphasizes civilian control over the armed forces.

DEFENSE BUDGET   Before the 1990s, grant aid from the Soviet Union constituted a significant percentage of Mongolia's defense budget. The cessation of Soviet aid and economic difficulties in Mongolia severely affected the defense budget, leading to yearly reductions. By 2000, the size of Mongolia's defense budget was seriously limited by the country's economic health. From 1998 to 2000, the Mongolian government kept the defense budget between 5.5 percent and 6.5 percent of total state budgetary expenditures and 1.9 percent–2.2 percent of GDP. In 2000, the defense budget structure consisted of seven categories. Table 1 shows the percentage changes in the budget for each of these categories. Table 2

Table 1. Distribution of Defense Budget Expenditures by Category, 1992–2000 (%)

	1992	1993	1994	1995	1996	1997	1998	1999	2000
Personnel salaries	29.0	16.0	27.0	34.0	35.0	27.0	33.5	41.6	45.2
Social provisions	31.0	25.0	26.0	24.0	20.0	34.7	27.7	27.6	26.7
Material provisions for personnel	30.0	50.0	38.0	35.0	37.0	20.0	22.0	23.0	21.0
Equipment rehabilitation	3.0	3.0	4.0	3.0	1.0	8.5	9.8	1.8	0.9
Training, cultural, and educational activities	3.0	2.0	2.0	3.0	3.0	3.0	3.0	3.0	3.5
Research and development	0.1	0.3	0.4	0.1	0.5	0.1	0.3	0.3	0.5
Other expenses	3.9	3.7	2.6	0.9	3.5	6.7	3.7	2.7	2.2
Total	100.0	100.0	100.0	100.0	100.0	100.0	100.0	100.0	100.0

SOURCE: Mongolian defense white paper 2000.

Table 2. Distribution of Defense Budget Expenditures by Personnel Group, 1996–2000 (%)

	1996	1997	1998	1999	2000
Commissioned and non-commissioned officers	49	41	42	50	54
Sergeants and soldiers	34	35	34	27	23
Civilian personnel	17	24	24	23	23

SOURCE: Mongolian defense white paper 2000.

shows the distribution of defense budget expenditures for personnel from 1996 to 2000 as a percentage of the total.

As can be seen in table 1, the government increased defense personnel salaries over the past seven years, indicating an emphasis on the welfare of military personnel. The share of military personnel salaries and benefits going to officers and noncommissioned officers increased to 54 percent, while salaries and benefits for those ranked sergeant and below dropped to 23 percent (table 2). The lack of financial resources for defense purposes created serious difficulties in equipment rehabilitation, research projects, military professionalization, and the increase of international exchanges for the armed forces.

CONTRIBUTIONS TO REGIONAL AND GLOBAL SECURITY

Mongolia seeks to take an active part in the prevention of armed aggression, the consolidation of bilateral and multilateral confidence-building activities, and the conduct of foreign policy to advance the country's vital national interests. In 1992, Mongolia declared its territory a nuclear-weapons-free zone. In December 1998, the UN General Assembly adopted a resolution entitled "Mongolia's International Security and Nuclear-Weapons-Free Status," welcoming Mongolia's nuclear-weapons-free status and inviting UN member states, including the five nuclear powers, to cooperate with Mongolia in implementing the resolution. In October 2000, the permanent members of the UN Security Council issued a statement granting security assurances to Mongolia in connection with its nuclear-weapons-free status.

In the Asia Pacific region, Mongolia attempts to make use of multilateral frameworks, such as the ASEAN Regional Forum (ARF), the Pacific Economic Cooperation Council (PECC), the Asia-Pacific Economic Cooperation (APEC) forum, and the Council for Security Cooperation in Asia Pacific (CSCAP). Although new to the ARF, Mongolia has already contributed to confidence building through hosting a meeting of the heads of regional defense colleges in September 1999. Mongolia has been active in a variety of other confidence-building measures, supporting the ARF's evolutionary approach and its function as a venue for discussing preventive diplomacy.

Although China and Russia have asked Mongolia to join the "Shanghai Five" grouping of China, Kazakhstan, the Kyrgyz Republic, Russia, and Tajikistan, Mongolia does not plan to do so. Mongolia sees the "Shanghai Five" as focused on the Islamic countries of Central Asia, an area in which Mongolia has no influence or vital concerns. However, Mongolia has expressed an interest in participating as an observer in several of the "Shanghai Five" group's activities, such as efforts to combat transnational crime and drug trafficking.

Mongolia is also concerned about unconventional security threats such as poverty, organized crime, drug trafficking, environmental degradation, and energy security. Mongolia encourages initiatives that take a closer look at the emerging concept of human security, especially track-two dialogues on regional security and cooperation. In May 2000, an international conference on Human Security in a Globalizing World was held in Ulaanbaatar. This conference generated a number of recommendations. UN Secretary General Kofi Annan hailed Mongolia's initiative in enhancing human security, and Mongolian Prime Minister Nambar Enkhbayer stressed the importance of cooperation by governments, nongovernmental organizations, private businesses, and individuals in achieving this goal. He also stressed that human rights and fundamental freedoms are of paramount importance to human security.

13 New Zealand

THE SECURITY ENVIRONMENT

New Zealand's security perceptions reflect its position as a small, wealthy, Western maritime nation, geographically distant from external conflicts. Although New Zealand faces perhaps fewer direct threats than any other country in the world, it relies heavily on overseas trade for its economic welfare. Merchant shipping carries more than 95 percent of New Zealand's exports and imports. Protecting shipping lanes is thus New Zealand's leading security interest. The other major interest is to contribute to the security of its largest trading partner, Australia, and the general stability of the Asia Pacific region.

As New Zealand heads into 2001, changes in the domestic political landscape are likely to generate new security challenges. The center-left government elected in late 1999 has initiated a reorientation in New Zealand's defense and security policy, raising concerns among New Zealand's established friends and allies.

INTERNAL   New Zealand entered the new millennium led by a newly elected center-left coalition government. Government ministers of this coalition emphatically argue that the cold war is over. In their view, cold war forms of security cooperation, such as the United States' alliance structure, undermine security and are hence no longer relevant to Asia Pacific in general and to New Zealand in particular. Following these arguments, the coalition government has initiated a radical change in defense policy that favors an army-dominated defense force trained and equipped for peacekeeping.

The radical shift in the coalition government's defense policy mirrors

118

a deep division in New Zealand on wider security and defense questions. All New Zealanders agree that their country faces no serious credible military threats in the short term. However, political parties, officials, and commentators and analysts are divided on what constitute longer-term threats to New Zealand.

Representatives from one side of this debate, who include coalition government ministers, center-left members of Parliament, and some academics and journalists, view the world as becoming more peaceful. They argue that military threats to the sovereignty of New Zealand are less likely in the future. Consequently, large investments in military hardware and technology, especially for the air force and navy, are unnecessary.

Proponents of this view also hold that conflict within nation-states is becoming more important than large-scale interstate conflict. Military forces thus should adapt to carry out humanitarian nonmilitary roles and peacekeeping. Finally, those on this side of the debate pay less attention to the strategic balance in Asia Pacific. Instead, smaller-scale humanitarian issues are emphasized, such as peacekeeping in East Timor and the South Pacific.

Interpreters from the other side of New Zealand's defense debate, represented by center-right members of Parliament, retired high-ranking military officers and government officials, as well as some journalists and academics, argue that history shows how strategic circumstances can change rapidly with unforeseen consequences. They believe interstate conflict is still important and point out that several of the world's most serious flash points for interstate conflict—the Korean peninsula, the Taiwan Strait, and the South China Sea—are located in the Asia Pacific region.

Consequently, advocates on this side of the debate argue that New Zealand should support the United States' positive contribution to regional security, strengthen its cooperative relations with like-minded states in the region, particularly Australia, Singapore, and Malaysia, and also work through regional mechanisms such as the ASEAN Regional Forum (ARF). New Zealand's involvement in multilateralism and peace-keeping is viewed as valuable. They also point out that if New Zealand wants to provide meaningful military contributions to international peacekeeping, it will need to make balanced investments in combat-capable armed forces.

EXTERNAL   Traditionally, New Zealand has sought to balance the promotion of global multilateralism with managing the real threats emanating from external developments. This has led New Zealand to cooperate closely with friends and allies, especially Australia, the United Kingdom, and the United States. However, in the mid-1980s Wellington banned the entry of nuclear armed or equipped ships from its ports, leading the United States to suspend its security guarantee to New Zealand under the Australia-New Zealand-United States defense alliance (ANZUS).

In response to various crises in the 1990s, New Zealand began to re-establish substantive defense cooperation with the United States, especially in peacekeeping. The United Nations–sanctioned International Force in East Timor (INTERFET) also strengthened the centrality of New Zealand's defense relationship with Australia. Both countries shared the burden of providing the bulk of combat forces to East Timor, with support from other like-minded states including France, Singapore, the United Kingdom, and the United States.

The trend toward New Zealand's strengthening ties with Australia and the United States came to an abrupt halt in 2000 as the newly elected center-left coalition government initiated its new approach to security. This approach raises questions about how New Zealand can inter-operate with its traditional defense partners and whether it intends to continue its stated defense responsibilities. Already during 2000, New Zealand's reputation as a reliable regional security contributor was called into question, reflected by Australia and the United States expressing concern with New Zealand's new direction in security and defense.

The New Zealand government rejected these concerns, warning Australia and the United States not to interfere in its internal defense affairs. The government went further and criticized the defense policies of Australia and the United States as inventing threats and excessively relying on technology. The New Zealand government also expressed concern directly to the United States over its theater missile defense (TMD) and national missile defense (NMD) proposals.

Changes in New Zealand's outward orientation have caused misgivings among its immediate neighbors as well. A greater emphasis on humanitarian and ethical issues in the country's foreign policy has led New Zealand to criticize openly many countries in the South Pacific. Most notably, Fiji was censured for civil rights shortcomings after an abortive coup led to the ouster of its democratically elected government. This stimulated a strong reaction from Fiji's interim government, which reduced to a minimum New Zealand's diplomatic access. As New Zealand enters 2001, its real influence may be declining in the South Pacific.

DEFENSE POLICIES AND ISSUES

DEFENSE POLICIES   In early 2000, the new coalition government signaled its intentions toward defense by canceling an agreement with the United States to lease-buy at low cost 28 F-16 aircraft. This move was defended by the argument that the F-16 was not relevant to peacekeeping since it was of little use in future conflicts, a legacy of the cold war, and an expensive investment in a capability that New Zealand had never used before.

New Zealand's chiefs of staff were excluded from this decision, although they provided evidence to an independent consultant of how this aircraft type could be used for peacekeeping and could deepen defense cooperation with regional allies. While the independent consultant accepted these arguments and recommended that the government purchase at least some of the aircraft, government officials stood by their decision, noting that the F-16 lease-buy agreement was canceled to avoid prejudging the outcome of a promised defense review.

However, soon afterward the government decided not to proceed with the defense review and instead issued a short, ten-page *Defense Policy Framework*, also without input from the armed services or other government agencies involved in defense and foreign policy. The framework was justified on the grounds that there was no need for a defense review as a parliamentary committee had already written an adequate defense report.

On the surface, the security and defense policies expressed in the *Defense Policy Framework* have much in common with the former conservative government's positions. The framework reiterates commitments to the defense of Australia, to regional security (especially the Five Power Defense Arrangements [FPDA] with Australia, Malaysia, Singapore, and the United Kingdom), to the security of the South Pacific, and to UN peacekeeping. However, the statement does not mention collaboration with the United States.

Notwithstanding these commitments, speeches and actions by coalition government ministers suggest an intention to distance defense policies from the past. Critics believe that ministers do not take seriously Australia's defense strategy that emphasizes defending its northern sea and air gap, or accept that sea and air control lie at the core of the FPDA. Ministers have also denied that sea and air control is a relevant aspect of peacekeeping, despite the important roles played by New Zealand's navy and air force in East Timor.

Besides the F-16 purchase, the coalition government also canceled several navy procurements, including a third surface combat warship and upgrades for New Zealand's six-ship Orion squadron. Some commentators see a distinct likelihood that New Zealand will disarm its air force. For their part, senior military, defense, and foreign affairs officials appear to know little about the government's intentions in defense policy.

DEFENSE BUDGET   In 2000, the coalition government upheld its promise not to cut defense spending. The defense budget even increased slightly to cover the East Timor contribution. However, the devaluation of the New Zealand dollar and higher fuel prices have increased the operating costs of the New Zealand Defense Force (NZDF). Therefore, defense spending, when assessed in U.S. dollar terms, has declined from US$824 million in 1999 to US$804 million in 2000. Moreover, defense spending as a percentage of gross domestic product declined from 1.1 percent in 1999 to around 1 percent in 2000, and in 2001 is expected to drop to below 1 percent for the first time.

The issue of defense spending is hotly contested in domestic debate. The government argues that if defense spending is to remain constant, then land forces should be favored because of their peacekeeping role. This rationale underpinned the government's decision to allocate almost all capital funds to the army in 2000. The army will benefit from the acquisition of 105 Light Armored Vehicles, new communications equipment, and light utility vehicles.

Critics argue that the navy, army, and air force all contribute to peacekeeping and defense missions in equally important ways and that New Zealand can afford to spend more on defense.

CONTRIBUTIONS TO REGIONAL AND GLOBAL SECURITY

During 2000, New Zealand continued close defense cooperation with Australia. NZDF from all three services exercised with the Australian Defense Force. A flight of New Zealand attack aircraft continued to be assigned to support the Royal Australian Navy.

New Zealand has also maintained its contribution to the UN-sanctioned peacekeeping force in East Timor, providing a light infantry battalion and utility helicopters. New Zealand's other direct contribution to security in Southeast Asia centered on the FPDA. In 2000, New

Zealand participated with warships and combat aircraft in the annual maritime-air exercises with Australia, Malaysia, Singapore, and the United Kingdom. In the South Pacific, New Zealand provided relevant military assistance to several nations, ranging from technical advice to maritime surveillance patrols. However, New Zealand suspended its military assistance to Fiji in 2000 to express its displeasure with political developments in that country.

At the global level, New Zealand has also continued its tradition of providing small numbers of military observers and staff officers to various peacekeeping operations throughout the world.

New Zealand's capacity to contribute to the defense of Australia and regional security arrangements in the future now appears uncertain, however. Its ability to participate significantly in peacekeeping operations is also increasingly in question. Specifically, it remains uncertain how New Zealand's small army can acquire operational skills for peacekeeping missions without the experience of training with close air support and heavy artillery. Future interoperability with traditional defense partners is also questionable due to neglect of international defense standardization agreements covering tactics, communications, and logistics. Consequently, some observers believe that New Zealand may risk isolating itself from the international defense mainstream.

14 Papua New Guinea

THE SECURITY ENVIRONMENT

In September 2000, Papua New Guinea celebrated 25 years as an independent nation. As one of a small number of postcolonial states to have maintained an unbroken record of democratic government, Papua New Guinea had some cause for satisfaction. However, there was also a widespread feeling that the country had not made the most of its opportunities and that, as it entered the 21st century, it faced a number of serious problems.

INTERNAL Following a change of government in July 1999, the incoming administration of Sir Mekere Morauta set about to address some of the problems it had inherited from previous governments. It introduced a new budget, initiated several economic and financial reforms, and reestablished amicable relations with the International Monetary Fund (IMF) and the World Bank. By early 2000, there was evidence that improved economic management was yielding returns, and the government's efforts received endorsement from international lenders and donors. The new government's commitment to restoring integrity to the institutions of state resulted in the initiation of several political reforms, including the passing of an Organic Law on the Integrity of Political Parties and Candidates, proposals to change the country's electoral system, and the stated intention to establish a National Anti-Corruption Agency.

In May 2000, Prime Minister Morauta declared that changes made in 1995 to the provincial government system were not working. Later in the year, he promised a new review of provincial government, withdrew powers from two provincial governments, and put a third on notice.

One of the provincial governments effectively suspended is located in the Southern Highlands, an area already marred by several years of inter-group ("tribal") fighting. The suspension of the provincial government has caused groups opposed to this move to threaten the operation of several large resource projects.

Elsewhere, *raskol* (criminal) activity and intergroup fighting pose a continuing problem for the delivery of government services and discourage both local and foreign investment. In Enga Province alone, it has been estimated that around 1,000 people have been killed in such fighting over the past four years. Intelligence sources in 2000 reported the widespread use of modern weapons in intergroup fighting and an ongoing trade in weapons from Australia and Indonesia, financed from the sale of marijuana.

In addition, morale within the Royal Papua New Guinea Constabulary is low and factionalism is rife. The ability of the Constabulary to contain tribal fighting appears to be declining, and over recent years the government has had to deal with substantial compensation demands for damages inflicted during police actions. Both Australia, through its aid agency AusAID, and the European Union (EU) have been assisting in programs designed to strengthen the capacity of the police force and the judiciary. In October 2000, a National Law and Justice Policy Plan, outlining measures designed to improve the law and justice sectors, was presented to Parliament.

The Bougainville Peace Process. Since the negotiation of a cease-fire on Bougainville in 1998, attempts to finally resolve the 12-year-old conflict have proceeded through a series of talks between the national government and Bougainville leaders and officials. The process suffered a setback when a Supreme Court decision in late 1999 effectively undermined the position of the Bougainville People's Congress (BPC)—the elected body that had been negotiating on behalf of Bougainvilleans with the national government. Consequently, a Bougainville Interim Provincial Government (BIPG) had to be created under the governorship of Bougainville Member of Parliament John Momis. A crisis was averted when it was agreed that the BPC would remain and support the BIPG in negotiations with the national government.

The talks during 2000 sought primarily to elaborate on the idea of "the highest form of autonomy" for Bougainville and to reach an agreement on weapons disposal. The presence in Bougainville of national security forces has been reduced to around 150–200 personnel, but this still constitutes a source of occasional tension. Also prominent on the agenda has been the Bougainvillean demand for a referendum on the future status of Bougainville, including the option of independence, something that has been ruled out by successive national governments.

In August 2000, Bougainville leaders expressed frustration at the slow progress of negotiations. Former Bougainville Revolutionary Army (BRA) leaders Sam Kauona and James Tanis even warned of a possible resumption of armed conflict. While the talks proceeded throughout the rest of the year, weapons disposal and the referendum remained sticking points. In October, the leader of the national government delegation at the time, former Prime Minister Sir Michael Somare, mentioned a plan to introduce a constitutional amendment to provide for a general referendum process. However, Somare was dropped in a December cabinet reshuffle. Talks resumed early in 2001, but the peace process remains fragile, with reports of growing support in Bougainville for hard-line leader Francis Ona.

EXTERNAL   In 1999, a Papua New Guinea Defense Force (PNGDF) white paper repeated the observation made previously that Papua New Guinea's geographic location places it in a relatively benign security environment. However, developments in Indonesia following the fall of President Suharto, particularly the growing separatist movement in Irian Jaya (West Papua), led the government to comment on "the essential frailty" of its security calculations. This reservation was further highlighted in 2000, first in May when a civilian-led coup in Fiji held members of the elected government hostage inside the Parliament, and then in June when the Solomon Islands' prime minister was taken captive by an armed group and subsequently forced to step down.

Successive Papua New Guinea governments have reiterated their support for Indonesian sovereignty over Irian Jaya. This policy was confirmed when Indonesia's Vice-President Megawati Sukarnoputri visited Papua New Guinea to attend the country's independence anniversary. In December, Prime Minister Morauta further emphasized that his government would "neither tolerate nor condone any action taken in Papua New Guinea by supporters of the independence movement in West Papua."

During 2000, the Papua New Guinea government arranged for the voluntary repatriation of around 700 West Papuans, most of whom had crossed into Papua New Guinea in the mid-1980s and had been resettled in Papua New Guinea's Western (Fly River) Province. Another 2,000 have been granted residence in Papua New Guinea. The Papua

New Guinea–Indonesia Border Liaison Committee, which met in Lae in August, also discussed repatriation arrangements and ways to facilitate travel between Vanimo and Jayapura.

While Papua New Guinea officially recognizes Indonesia's sovereignty in Irian Jaya, many Papua New Guineans sympathize with West Papuan independence demands. In 2000, these elements urged the Papua New Guinea government to follow the lead of the Pacific Island states Vanuatu and Nauru in supporting West Papuan demands for a review of the 1969 "Act of Free Choice" by which Indonesia incorporated West Papua. In June, the governor of Papua New Guinea's Sandaun (West Sepik) Province, John Tekwie, was expelled from Irian Jaya because he attended a West Papuan congress in Jayapura. Moreover, young Papua New Guineans are reported to have crossed the border to support West Papuan separatists.

Toward the end of 2000, the Indonesian government appeared to be reversing its policy of tolerating greater expressions of West Papuan identity (for example, accepting a name change from "Irian Jaya" to "Papua," and allowing the West Papuan flag to be flown). At the time of these changes, sightings of Indonesian troops were reported on the Papua New Guinea side of the border and some 300 Papuans sought refuge in Papua New Guinea. In early December, Papua New Guinea increased patrols in the border area.

Should Indonesia revert to a hard line against West Papuan nationalism, renewed activity by the Organisasi Papua Merdeka (OPM), or the Free Papua Movement, is likely. This might also lead to a greater flow of refugees into Papua New Guinea. In an interview with an Australian newspaper in August 2000, Prime Minister Morauta voiced fears that Papua New Guinea could be "sucked into" a conflict between the OPM and the Indonesian military. Clearly, increased unrest in West Papua would be unwelcome in Papua New Guinea. The country has enjoyed cordial relations with Indonesia for more than a decade and, according to a statement by Defense Minister Muki Taranupi in September 2000, currently lacks the capacity to patrol the border.

The May 2000 coup in Fiji had little direct impact on Papua New Guinea. However, many commentators saw developments in Fiji as having inspired the subsequent "coup" in the Solomon Islands. The Solomons coup prodded Prime Minister Morauta to express "serious concern" at the capture of his Solomons counterpart, Bartholomew Ulufa'alu. While acknowledging that the incident was a domestic matter, Morauta condemned the group responsible, the Malaita Eagle

Force, and offered support for a constitutional resolution to the conflict. Reports also implicated the BRA in a raid in the western Solomons. Although these reports were denied by the BRA, the Papua New Guinea government stated that it would not allow its territory to be used as a base for attacks against neighboring countries.

In October 2000, peace talks in Townsville, Australia, led to an agreement by the main parties to the Solomon Islands conflict. However, it is far from certain whether this will end the hostilities. If the conflict persists, serious security implications would result for Papua New Guinea. First, Bougainvilleans have historically maintained close ties to the Solomon Islands, garnering political support from former Prime Minister Solomon Mamaloni and using the islands as a base for supplies, medical care, and weapons procurement. These ties could draw some Bougainvilleans into a Solomons conflict. Second, separatist demands have intermittently been voiced in the western Solomon Islands, which share a border with Papua New Guinea. If the conflict between the main islands of Malaita and Guadalcanal resumes, the Western Breakaway Movement could gain strength and seek support from Papua New Guineans. Finally, around 300–350 Papua New Guinea citizens reside in the Solomon Islands. Evacuation arrangements were made for them in June, though at least one Papua New Guinean was killed during fighting in Honiara.

Following the previous government's flirtation with recognizing Taiwan, the Morauta government moved during 2000 to consolidate relations with the People's Republic of China. In March, PNGDF officials signed a second memorandum of understanding, under which China pledged some K1.2 million (US$368,098 at US$1 = K3.26) of logistical (noncombat equipment) assistance to the PNGDF. In August, the deputy chief of staff of the People's Liberation Army (PLA) visited Port Moresby. During the same month, Foreign Minister Sir John Kaputin met his counterpart, Tang Jiaxuan, in China. Shortly after Kaputin's visit, the government announced that China would provide K3.3 million (US$1.01 million) for the construction of a new Department of Foreign Affairs building in Port Moresby.

DEFENSE POLICIES AND ISSUES

The PNGDF white paper tabled in Parliament in 1999 spelled out Papua New Guinea's defense doctrine and policies. The white paper recommended a smaller, more mobile and capable force. Rather than internal security, it emphasized the defense of Papua New Guinea's sovereignty, regional security arrangements, and nation building.

While the incoming Morauta government endorsed the policy positions set forth in the white paper, it did little during 2000 to implement the recommendations. This lack of decisive action was reflected by continued low morale in the PNGDF, with several incidents suggesting poor discipline. In early 2000, soldiers staged an angry protest outside the Ministry of Defense demanding a 100 percent pay raise (they eventually received 5 percent). In September, as Papua New Guinea's 25th anniversary of independence was celebrated, soldiers at the Moem Barracks in Wewak, East Sepik Province, went on a rampage, forcing Papua New Guinean and Indonesian dignitaries to flee. The following week about 100 soldiers marched on the Port Moresby General Hospital to retrieve the body of a colleague shot dead by police following an armed holdup. Rocks were thrown and a police vehicle set alight. Rumors that soldiers were about to march on the National Parliament building forced the legislative body to postpone its session.

These incidents prompted the formation of a parliamentary task force on defense headed by Defense Minister Taranupi. Introducing the task force's report to Parliament in October, Prime Minister Morauta spoke of a "culture of instability" in the PNGDF and commented that the institutional breakdown of the force was the result of years of neglect and mismanagement. The report itself argued that the basic needs of the PNGDF had not been met, that management was not working, and that the purpose, capacity, and resources of the PNGDF needed to be examined.

As a result of this report, the prime minister indicated his intention to carry out a "radical overhaul" of the PNGDF, raising the possibility of creating a coast guard–type air and maritime service and a highly mobile specialist unit, "the latter possibly as part of the police." Suggestions were made to reduce force size from 4,200 to 1,500 by mid-2001. After talks with Australia, an increase in Australian support for the PNGDF under the Defense Co-operation Program from A$8 million (US$4.4 million at A$1 = US$0.55) to A$25 million (US$13.75 million) was announced, including the provision of up to 30 defense advisers. The bulk of Australia's financial assistance will be a one-time payment to enable the PNGDF to pay entitlements owed to soldiers, meet outstanding debts, and cover downsizing costs. Australia also offered to extend the assistance provided through its Pacific Patrol Boat program.

Moreover, support to the Defense Department is anticipated from the World Bank. Budget estimates show a modest increase in defense spending from K85.1 million (US$26.1 million) in fiscal year 2000 to K90.4 million (US$27.73 million) in fiscal 2001.

The proposed review of the PNGDF will be the latest in a series of reviews and white papers. So far there has been little follow-through on earlier reviews. However, with Papua New Guinea's external security environment deteriorating, the Morauta government might show a greater resolve than its predecessors.

CONTRIBUTIONS TO REGIONAL AND GLOBAL SECURITY

With a population of around 4.5 million, Papua New Guinea is a minor actor on the world stage. Nonetheless, it has participated in a variety of international fora and has been outspoken particularly on matters concerning human rights and the environment. Substantial cuts to the country's foreign affairs budget (from K29 million [US$8.89 million] in 1999 to K18 million [US$5.52 million] in 2000) have forced Papua New Guinea to reduce its overseas representation. Allegations of irregularities in the issuing of passports have also prompted a major review of the Foreign Affairs Department. The report from this review is expected in early 2001.

Papua New Guinea has played an active role as a member of the Melanesian Spearhead Group and the Pacific Islands Forum (including its Regional Security Committee). In a communiqué from the Pacific Islands Forum meeting held in October 2000 in Kiribati, the 16 members welcomed measures to restore peace and democracy in Fiji and the Solomon Islands. The communiqué also expressed "deep concern" over past and recent violence in Irian Jaya and called on the Indonesian government and West Papuan leaders (four of whom attended the meeting) to resolve their differences through dialogue and consultation. Finally, the forum endorsed a plan that committed members to promote democratic governance.

Developments in Fiji and the Solomon Islands during 2000 gave added importance to Papua New Guinea's regional role. South Pacific Forum nations attending the joint assembly of the European Union and the African, Caribbean, and Pacific Group of States (ACP Group) in Benin condemned the illegal overthrow of democratically elected governments, while acknowledging that "the solution to the crisis is a domestic matter for Fiji and the Solomons." The meeting resolved to send a small ministerial mission led by PNG Foreign Minister Kaputin to look at the situation in Fiji and the Solomons and advise the ACP-EU joint assembly on possible responses. Kaputin's report was presented in Brussels in October. Papua New Guinea has also provided financial assistance to the Solomon Islands (K40 million [US$12.26 million] was committed in 1998 to be paid over four years), in part to support the Royal Solomon Islands Police Force.

Papua New Guinea is a signatory to the Treaty of Amity and Cooperation of the Association of Southeast Asian Nations (ASEAN) and a participant in the ASEAN Regional Forum (ARF) and the Asia-Pacific Economic Cooperation (APEC) forum; the country is also represented in the nongovernmental Council for Security and Cooperation in Asia Pacific (CSCAP). Papua New Guinea sees itself as providing a bridge between Southeast Asia and the island Pacific. Reacting to ASEAN's (and specifically Singapore's) reluctance to expand its membership eastwards, Indonesia's President Abdurrahman Wahid has proposed the creation of a new regional body, a West Pacific Forum, which would include Papua New Guinea as well as Australia, East Timor, Indonesia, New Zealand, and possibly the Philippines.

15 Philippines

THE SECURITY ENVIRONMENT

The Philippines faces more difficult challenges in 2001 than in the previous year. Although the economy showed signs of improving in early 2000, the Mindanao conflict and scandals plaguing the Estrada administration led to political instability, making a full economic recovery difficult and ultimately forcing President Joseph Estrada's resignation in early 2001. The kidnapping of foreign nationals in Malaysian resorts by the Abu Sayaf Group (ASG) embarrassed the Philippine government internationally. These developments may compel the Philippines to be more inward looking in the next several years, possibly making it a less active regional player.

DOMESTIC POLITICS   Controversies and scandals plagued the Estrada administration. At the beginning of the year 2000, the chair of the Securities and Exchange Commission accused President Estrada of exerting pressure to exonerate a presidential friend and campaign contributor accused of stock manipulation and insider trading. This controversy marked the start of an unabated decline in the stock market. Even the passage in July of a new Securities Regulation Code that provides stringent disclosure rules and stiffer penalties for insider trading could not stop the weakening of the market.

In October, a longtime friend of President Estrada, the provincial governor of Ilocos, Sur Luis Singson, revealed that between November 1998 and August 2000 he had delivered to Estrada more than P400 million (US$8.01 million at US$1 = P49.90) collected from an illegal numbers game called *jueteng*. He also disclosed that he had given the president P130 million (US$2.6 million) from his province's share of tobacco excise taxes. Subsequently, a resolution to impeach President Estrada was filed and approved by the House of Representatives. At the end of 2000, the impeachment trial began in the Senate, but the outcome was decided in the streets.

The political instability resulting from the Estrada scandals further intensified the stock market's decline and led the Philippine peso to slump to its lowest value of less than P55 to the U.S. dollar. Despite new leadership (Gloria Macapagal Arroyo is a professional economist), the economy will likely face difficulties in recovering.

THE ECONOMY   During the first quarter of 2000, the Philippine economy appeared to be recovering, with gross domestic product growing by 3.4 percent, surpassing the 1.2 percent growth rate during the same period in 1999. However, the Mindanao conflict and the political crisis forced the government to lower its projected GDP growth rate of 4 percent for 2000. Government statistics also indicate that inflation is rising, primarily as a result of oil price increases and the peso's depreciation. Unemployment has also risen, reaching 13.9 percent by June 2000. The government budget deficit for 2000 had reached P130 billion (US$2.6 billion), well above the P62 billion (US$1.24 billion) target for the full year.

INTERNAL SECURITY   Driven primarily by lingering poverty in the countryside, Muslim secessionists and communist insurgents continue to thrive and challenge government authority. In 2000, the Moro Islamic Liberation Front (MILF) posed the greatest military challenge. The government had reached an agreement with the MILF for a general cessation of hostilities in 1997 and opened formal peace talks in 1999. However, because the MILF attacked military detachments, blockaded national roads, and occupied villages, President Estrada declared an all-out military offensive against the group in 2000. The Armed Forces of the Philippines (AFP) drove the MILF from the villages it occupied and retook MILF camps, including the MILF's main camp, Abubakar, in early July. Despite these military successes, some Philippine commentators criticized the military offensive, arguing that the MILF insurgency can only be solved by sustained development in Mindanao.

Although the MILF ceded territory, it remains formidable with an estimated 15,233 fighters, only 457 less than at the end of 1999. The AFP offensive in Mindanao was expensive. More than P1 billion (US$20 million) was spent, with estimates of daily expenditures ranging from P10 million (US$200,400) to P20 million (US$400,800). In addition, more than 200 soldiers were killed and several hundred wounded. The fighting also killed more than 200 civilians and displaced around 140,000 families.

During the conflict, the MILF tried to garner external support by sending representatives to the Organization of the Islamic Conference (OIC) meeting held in Malaysia in mid-2000. The MILF's action was endorsed by Nur Misuari, the leader of the Moro National Liberation Front (MNLF), a rival rebel group that the OIC recognizes as the sole representative of the Moro people. The OIC eventually asked the Philippine government and the MILF to stop their fighting and prepared to send a team of observers to examine the situation in Mindanao.

Meanwhile, the ASG grew from an estimated 1,157 fighters in 1999 to approximately 2,000 by the middle of 2000. The financial rewards generated by kidnapping foreigners lured new recruits. In late March, one faction kidnapped 53 persons, including teachers and students. Several hostages were later released, and some were rescued by the military. However, four persons, including a priest, were tortured and killed. In April, another ASG faction crossed over to Malaysia's diving resort of Sipadan and took several foreign nationals as hostages to Mindanao's Jolo Island. The same group later kidnapped 13 Christian evangelists and three French journalists.

Initially, the Philippine government negotiated for the hostages' release. Later, several concerned European governments asked Libya to negotiate on their behalf (based on Libya's connections with the Islamic groups). At this point, the Philippine government refused to pay any ransom, generating friction between Philippine and Libyan negotiators. In late August, however, the Philippine government confirmed that the ASG had received around P245 million (US$4.9 million) for hostages previously released, opening the door to ransom negotiations. The ASG demanded US$25 million for the remaining mostly foreign hostages, including US$12 million in so-called developmental aid from Libya.

Following the first abductions of foreign nationals from Malaysia, another ASG faction kidnapped three Malaysians from Malaysia's Pandanan Island in September. This prompted President Estrada to declare an all-out military offensive against the ASG. Subsequently, the three French journalists, 13 evangelists, and the three Malaysians taken from Pandanan Island were found. However, one American and one Filipino taken from Sipadan remain captives as military operations continue.

The ASG's kidnappings caused the Philippines international embarrassment. Fortunately, the incident did not undermine Philippine-Malaysian relations, but rather encouraged greater border patrol cooperation. The Philippines suggested a trilateral border agreement, building on existing bilateral agreements between Malaysia and Indonesia.

The Mindanao conflict also prompted Manila to postpone elections for the Autonomous Region in Muslim Mindanao (ARMM) to May 2001. MNLF leader Misuari, who also acts as the governor of the ARMM, threatened to resume fighting if the government failed to fulfill its obligations under the 1996 Peace Agreement that it had signed with the MNLF. Despite his threats, Misuari stayed on as governor.

Besides Muslim insurgents in the south, communist insurgents also pose a major security threat. The Philippine Defense Department estimated communist insurgents to number about 10,600 at the end of 1999, 18 percent more than in 1998. These insurgents continue to attack military and police installations. They also hold one military and one police officer hostage.

FOREIGN POLICY AND EXTERNAL SECURITY   At the end of 2000, territorial disputes in the South China Sea remained a major external concern for the Philippines. Early in the year, Chinese fishing vessels were sighted around the contested Scarborough Shoal near the Philippine province of Zambales. These vessels were reportedly carrying coral and "construction materials," prompting the Philippine navy to give chase. The Philippine government also filed diplomatic protests with China.

In March 2000, China finally endorsed the code of conduct for the South China Sea proposed in 1999. This code covers the handling of disputes, consultation modes, confidence-building measures, and agreements on environmental protection. China's signing of the code helped stabilize the situation in the South China Sea just as the AFP initiated a campaign against the MILF in Mindanao. Simultaneously dealing with troubles in the South China Sea and Mindanao would have been extremely difficult for the AFP. In addition, while dealing with China on issues related to the code of conduct, the Philippines also undertook confidence-building measures with other countries, the most recent being the second Joint Marine Scientific Survey with Vietnam.

In Southeast Asia, the Philippine government is particularly concerned about the situation in Indonesia, especially religious conflicts in Maluku and Ambon, militias in East and West Timor, and the bomb attack in 2000 on the Philippine ambassador's residence in Jakarta. The Philippines, remembering Indonesia's assistance in forging the 1996 Peace Agreement with the MNLF, hopes that Indonesia can continue to provide a key leadership role in the Association of Southeast Asian Nations (ASEAN).

During 2000, relations with the United States continued to improve. With the approval of the Visiting Forces Agreement in 1999, large-scale military exercises between Philippine and U.S. forces resumed. From January to March 2000, approximately 2,500 U.S. personnel and an equal number of AFP troops participated in the Balikatan Exercise.

Furthermore, a defense experts group comprising Philippine and U.S. defense officials was formed to "regularly discuss and assess military equipment that the United States could provide the Philippines." Finally, the U.S. Congress authorized the "transfer of Excess Defense Articles to the Philippines," including US$5 million in foreign military financing for the years 2000 and 2001.

When President Estrada visited the United States in July, he was able to secure approximately US$105 million worth of military equipment, US$20 million in food aid for Mindanao, and expanded medical and health benefits for Filipino war veterans. The U.S. secretary of defense also visited the Philippines, where he assured Philippine officials of U.S. support for the AFP's campaign against the MILF.

DEFENSE POLICIES AND ISSUES

PRIORITIES The Philippines' national defense priorities and strategy are unchanged from the previous year (see *Asia Pacific Security Outlook 2000*). Defense priorities include internal security, regional stability, and force modernization. The five-point strategy is summarized as "Defend-Respond-Build-Promote-Prepare."

DEFENSE STRATEGY For external defense, the Philippine government focuses on two strategies: first, the strategy of total defense, which mobilizes all Filipinos and resources for the defense of the Philippines; and second, the principle of active defense, which identifies potential sources of threat at the earliest possible time through political and diplomatic means. For internal defense, the Philippine government uses the total approach strategy, which requires military and civilian agencies to undertake concerted efforts to address insurgencies.

MODERNIZATION AND PROCUREMENT In 1995, the Philippine Congress authorized the modernization of the AFP. However, no notable improvement in the AFP's equipment and capability for external defense has developed. The 1997 financial crisis forced the government to suspend procurements. Thereafter, the reappearance of insurgencies led to the reprioritization of equipment purchases. New procurements are now oriented toward internal security operations. Nonetheless, although the president released P5.5 billion (US$110 million) for equipment acquisitions, no procurements have taken place due to tedious bureaucratic procedures.

DEFENSE BUDGET Even including the expenses for the military campaign against the MILF, the Philippines has one of the lowest defense budgets in the region, relative to the national budget and gross national product. The defense budget covers the AFP as well as civilian agencies under the Department of National Defense.

The total defense budget for fiscal year 2000 was P53.6 billion (US$1.07 billion), which constituted only 8 percent of the national budget (of P629 billion, or US$12.60 billion) and approximately 1.5 percent of projected GNP. The AFP budget was P41 billion (US$821 million), 6.5 percent of the national budget and approximately 1.15 percent of projected GNP.

Of the fiscal 2000 AFP budget, 78.9 percent went to personnel services, 20.6 percent to maintenance of weapons and equipment, and only 0.4 percent to capital outlay (down from 1 percent the previous year). By component, the army received 32.16 percent of the 2000 budget, the air force 13.45 percent, the navy 16.86 percent, and general headquarters 10.27 percent.

INTERNAL SECURITY OPERATIONS Due to the flaring up of insurgency in Mindanao, internal security operations have become the primary focus of the AFP, a situation that is likely to continue in the near term. During the campaign against the MILF, more than half of the AFP's ground forces were stationed in Mindanao. And after the fall of the MILF's main camp in July, the AFP through its corps of engineers helped to reconstruct and repair damaged infrastructure in Mindanao.

The return of insurgency in the Philippines prodded the government to reactivate paramilitary forces. This created worries in some sectors because paramilitary forces have been responsible for human rights violations in the past. President Estrada also directed the AFP to become more involved in police and civilian-led activities to curb crime.

CONTRIBUTIONS TO REGIONAL AND GLOBAL SECURITY

REGIONAL   In 2000, the Philippines continued to actively participate in regional institutions. Despite the political crisis in the Philippines, President Estrada attended the Asia-Pacific Economic Cooperation (APEC) summit in Brunei in November. In the Asia-Europe Meeting (ASEM), the Philippines helped direct the implementation of the ASEM Trade Facilitation Action Plan. The Philippines also continued to participate in track-two efforts for security and economic cooperation in the region, specifically in the Council for Security Cooperation in Asia Pacific (CSCAP) and the Pacific Economic Cooperation Council (PECC).

In 2000, the Philippines established diplomatic relations with North Korea. Pyongyang had assured the Philippines in 1999 that it would participate in the ASEAN Regional Forum (ARF) if Manila agreed to normalize relations. The Philippines' recognition of Pyongyang thus helped pave the way for North Korea's participation in the ARF meeting in July.

BILATERAL RELATIONS   High-level visits are a principal mechanism for enhancing the Philippines' bilateral ties. President Estrada visited China, Japan, and the United States during the year. On his visit to China, Estrada and China's President Jiang Zemin agreed to pursue the peaceful settlement of disputes in the South China Sea and promised to maintain peace and stability in the area. They also witnessed the signing of a Joint Statement on the Framework of Bilateral Cooperation in the 21st Century, which "seeks to prevent conflicts in the region arising from territorial disputes."

GLOBAL   The United Nations continues to be the Philippines' main channel for contributing to global security. The Philippines sent troops to UN peacekeeping operations in East Timor. The appointment of a Filipino, Lieutenant General Jaime de los Santos, to act as head of the UN peacekeeping force in East Timor provided the Philippines a rare opportunity to contribute directly to peace and stability in the region. And despite severe domestic financial constraints, the Philippines contributed US$200,000 to the Humanitarian Assistance Fund for East Timor and US$250,000 to the United Nations Mission in East Timor (UNAMET) Trust Fund.

Besides its activities in UN peacekeeping, the Philippines is also a member of several UN bodies, including the International Maritime Organization Council, the United Nations Educational, Scientific, and Cultural Organization (UNESCO) Executive Board, and the UN Commission on Human Rights. The Philippines also actively participated in the preparatory process for the February 2000 UN Conference on Trade and Development (UNCTAD) meeting in Bangkok.

Finally, the Philippines remains committed to promoting democracy. In support of this objective, in mid-September 2000 the Philippines hosted a meeting of leaders of democratic societies.

16 Russia

The Security Environment

With the resignation of President Boris Yeltsin on New Year's Eve 1999 and the election of Vladimir Putin as Russia's second president in March 2000, a new era has begun in Russian politics. Externally, this era is marked by the realization that for Russia a period of a half millennium as a largely self-contained, self-sustained universe has come to an end. In other words, the period of Russia as a Eurasian empire is finally over. Now Russia is making the transition to a middle power, ever more closely tied to the European Union (EU) and progressively concerned with its southern and eastern flanks. This transition is fraught with manifold tensions between bold steps toward the future and reactionary reversals.

Internally, Putin's presidency is characterized by a fresh emphasis on the role of the state, which was severely weakened in the preceding decade of post-Communist transformation. Putin evidently seeks to combine political conservatism with economic liberalism, Russian patriotism with the search for foreign investments, and the reduction of the role of autonomous power centers (regional authorities, business tycoons, and the independent media) with what he terms the "dictatorship of law." In the future, Putin's vision of Russia might either evolve in the direction of a genuine rule of law or push the country toward a dictatorship.

Putin's policies are officially guided by a set of documents adopted early in his tenure. This conceptual framework includes the National Security Concept (January 2000), the Military Doctrine (April 2000), the Foreign Policy Concept (July 2000), the Information Security Concept (September 2000), and several other policy papers. Rather than setting priorities and agendas for the government in their respective areas, these blueprints are mainly philosophical in spirit and bureaucratic (rather than political) in nature. From the standpoint of operational planning, they contribute little, but they do propose interesting tools with which to analyze the evolution of Russian political and strategic thinking.

INTERNAL   Clearly, Putin's vision of Russia is more inward looking, concentrating on Russia's plethora of internal problems. The new president's first state-of-the-nation address in July 2000 stressed the importance of economics and demographics, and barely mentioned traditional national security issues. To "make Russia strong," in Putin's view, means above all helping the economy to become viable and attractive for would-be investors. A major prerequisite for this is ensuring the domestic stability of the country.

To enhance the internal unity of Russia, Putin has launched a reform of the federation that aims to reduce the power of regional governors who in the past had frequently defied the federal Constitution. In particular, the governors have lost their seats on the Federation Council, the upper chamber of the Russian parliament. To strengthen the power of the presidency, Putin has divided the country into seven macro-regions, each headed by a Kremlin representative. The boundaries of these new territories often coincide with those of the military districts. Five out of seven representatives are army or security services generals.

The purpose of this reform is to do away with the "feudal federation" of the 1990s, which made regional chiefs virtually independent inside their territories and allowed them to act as influential power brokers in Moscow. The changes seek to raise the level of Russia's governability, and the choice of military officers (rather than politicians) as the Kremlin's representatives should guarantee their personal loyalty to Putin. Faced with the president's strong resolve, the governors have so far refused to challenge the changes. If, however, Putin's attempt to relaunch Russia's economy should fail, his power base shrink, and his popularity decline, the regional barons may try to reassert themselves in the future. Ironically, the seven macro-regions, conceived as a tool for keeping Russia together, may hypothetically present a pattern for the country's ultimate disintegration.

Against this background, the issue of military reform came to the fore for the first time since the 1998 financial crisis. Initially, this was provoked by a rare public row between Defense Minister Igor Sergeyev and Chief of the General Staff Anatoly Kvashnin. Whereas Sergeyev, a former missile expert, stressed the importance of the strategic nuclear arsenal as the mainstay of Russia's defense posture, Kvashnin, an ex-commander of the North Caucasus military district, proposed drastic cuts of strategic arms (to below 1,000 weapons) and the phasing out of the Strategic Rocket Forces (SRF) as an independent service.

A meeting of the Russian Security Council in August 2000 failed to resolve the differences. Soon afterward the nuclear-powered submarine *Kursk* sank in the Barents Sea. The agony that accompanied the ill-fated rescue effort severely damaged the credibility of the entire defense establishment, including the president as commander-in-chief, and made it clear that the Russian military needed a major overhaul, emphasizing quality over quantity. In the fall of 2000, it was announced that the Russian Armed Forces (whose authorized strength is 1.2 million and actual number of servicemen just above 1 million) and "other troops" (whose combined strength is around half a million) would see personnel cuts of 350,000–365,000 by 2003, encompassing 180,000 in the army, 50,000 in the navy, and 40,000 in the air force. The Interior Troops of the Ministry of the Interior are expected to be reduced by more than 20,000; the Railroad Troops by 10,000; and the Frontier Guards by 5,000. Ten other government agencies that have military formations organic to them should see reductions of more than 25,000 servicemen. Most importantly, the number of general officers will be cut from 1,500 to 1,000, and the Ministry of Defense central staff will be limited to 10,000. This massive downsizing, driven by financial constraints, is already meeting with stiff opposition and will not come easily.

Internal security also remains challenged by continued fighting in the North Caucasus. Although the "military phase" of the war in Chechnya was announced over in April 2000, Chechen rebels, who are still engaged in guerrilla warfare with the Russian military and police, have proved difficult to suppress. The majority of the Russian people, however, continue to support the government on Chechnya but without enthusiasm. In a single year of the second Chechen war (October 1999–September 2000), the number of Russian military casualties exceeded 2,700 dead and 9,000 wounded, while Chechen forces are reported to have lost between 13,000 and 14,000 men. The official cost of the war effort is put at R5 billion (US$177 million at US$1 = R28.16) for 1999 and R6 billion (US$213 million) for the first three months of 2000. Some independent estimates run to R32.5 billion (US$1.1 billion). Rebuilding Chechnya may cost R7.5 billion (US$266 million) in 2000 and as much as R30 billion–R42 billion (US$1.06 billion–US$1.49 billion) in

2001. Still, the prospects for political stabilization and economic and social rehabilitation in the region are dim. Under these conditions, the war is likely to drag on, and may even become more intense.

EXTERNAL Putin's "Russia project"—ensuring political stability and reviving the economy—calls for Western investments and technology transfers. Thus, foreign policy in Russia is increasingly seen as a resource for domestic economic development. When Putin became president, fears of another cold war were widespread. Yet, while making clear he had no ties with Washington, Putin has consciously abstained from confrontation with the United States and worked to improve the relationship. During the February 2000 visit to Moscow by North Atlantic Treaty Organization (NATO) Secretary-General George Robertson, relations with the alliance, suspended in the wake of the Kosovo crisis, were partially restored. In April 2000, the Russian parliament ratified the Strategic Arms Reduction Treaty 2 (START-2), something it had refused to do for seven years under Boris Yeltsin. Finally, summit-level dialogue became more intense as President Bill Clinton paid his last official visit to Russia less than a month after Putin's inauguration.

Nevertheless, Russia refused to compromise on the Anti-Ballistic Missile (ABM) Treaty and made no significant concessions to the West, especially on the Chechnya issue. To counter U.S. plans to build a national missile defense (NMD) system, Putin used a three-pronged strategy. Together with the Chinese, Russia loudly protested against the NMD; to the Europeans, Putin offered a theater missile defense (TMD) system with Russian participation and invited the United States to join; and to the Americans, Moscow offered to cooperate on the boost-phase intercept ballistic missile defense system. Despite a cool reception from Europe and the United States, Russia used this strategy to buy time with the outgoing Clinton administration as it anticipated dealing with the next U.S. president.

Ultimately, Moscow feels confident about the effectiveness of its nuclear deterrent. An agreement to modify the ABM Treaty that would accommodate Russian and U.S. security concerns in the field of strategic stability is feasible, and certainly much more likely than a return to lasting confrontation. In this context, opposition to U.S. plans for a TMD system in East Asia is less an expression of Russia's own security worries than a result of Russia's relationship with China. Nonetheless, the possible chain reaction in Asia to Russia's efforts to counter the U.S. NMD should be cause for concern in Moscow.

Refusing to build his foreign policy on mere reactions to U.S. moves, Putin also has sought to improve relations with countries in the European Union. Putin's principal interest regarding the European Union is how its expansion to the east (e.g., the terms of trade with Central and Eastern European countries; the new visa restrictions on Russian visitors to those countries; and the special issue of Kaliningrad) might affect Russia and the future of the European security and defense identity. In this regard, one breakthrough was achieved in the fall of 2000 when Russia and the European Union agreed to build an "energy partnership" calling for a vast expansion of Russian gas shipments to EU countries coupled with Western European investments in the Russian energy sector. Clearly, as Russia exits from its relative isolation, sheds the remnants of superpower mentality, and looks for ways to integrate into a wider world, the importance of Europe for Russia's foreign policy is likely to grow.

Central Asia. If Europe is largely perceived to be an opportunity, Central Asia has been marked out as a "clear and present danger." Putin has spoken of a belt of instability stretching from Kosovo to the Philippines. In fact, Russian officials have even suggested that their country was becoming a shield of the civilized world from the onslaught of Islamic extremism. "International terrorism" was identified as an enemy threatening Russia in the North Caucasus and its allies in Central Asia, and the Afghan Taliban were accused of aiding and abetting these terrorists.

Moscow's strategy for standing up to instability in Central Asia includes strengthening politico-military ties with Uzbekistan and Russian allies in the Collective Security Treaty (CST)—Kazakhstan, the Kyrgyz Republic, and Tajikistan; putting Russian troops in Tajikistan on alert; dedicating a 50,000-strong force for missions in the area; reaching out to China, India, and the United States, whose interests are also affected; and, finally, applying military and diplomatic pressure on the Taliban.

This strategy, however, misses the central point: the source of instability is not foreign subversion but rather the failure of state- and nation-building in several of the former Soviet republics. This has produced social protest wrapped in Islamic colors, internal separatist movements, and rivalries between the newly independent states. In the foreseeable future, relations with the Moslem world on Russia's periphery and inside the federation are likely to remain among Moscow's principal worries.

Asia Pacific. Putin's arrival in the Kremlin has marked an intensification of Russia's Asia policy. In reality, this policy begins at home, in Siberia and the Russian Far East. Putin has made several trips to the area, sounding alarm over the demographic trend of declining populations threatening Russia's entire position east of the Urals. The president has stressed the need for keeping the Russian population in place, developing the region's technological and scientific potential, building energy links to Asian countries, and attracting foreign investment and technology to the region. The future of Siberia and the Russian Far East is now understood to be the supreme geopolitical challenge facing Russia as it enters the 21st century. This challenge also creates the domestic rationale for developing ties with Asia Pacific.

During the year 2000, contacts with China were further deepened at bilateral, regional (e.g., Central Asian), and global levels. Summit meetings have become more frequent, and the relationship at that level is more engaged. Russia and China continue to vigorously support the ABM Treaty, and they condemn U.S. plans for building NMD and TMD systems in East Asia. (Interestingly, Putin's European TMD initiative was not cleared with Beijing). On the economic front, ties with China continue to stagnate while arms sales and technology transfers are booming.

To better balance Russia's Asia policy, Putin has become personally involved in relations with Japan. Although the territorial dispute over the southern Kuril Islands remains unresolved, Moscow and Tokyo have managed to move beyond the 2000 deadline for their peace treaty. Some patterns for security cooperation are emerging and political contacts are intense, while economic interaction largely depends on the progress of Russian domestic reforms.

Russia has also taken significant steps to become a more active player on the Korean peninsula. In July 2000, Putin made the first-ever visit to Pyongyang by any Russian or Soviet leader. Immediately aimed at withdrawing the rationale for U.S. NMD plans, the trip paved the way to a new trilateral relationship between Moscow, Seoul, and Pyongyang with high-level contacts among the three capitals intensifying.

Finally, India has started to figure more prominently in Russia's foreign policy strategy. A declaration on strategic partnership was signed in New Delhi during Putin's visit there (the first by a Russian president in seven and a half years) in October 2000. Despite its broad implications, the current foundation for the bilateral relationship remains very shallow, centered on Russian arms and technology transfers to India.

The latest batch, worth over US$5 billion, includes an aircraft carrier (*Admiral Gorshkov*), SU-30 MKI fighters, T-90 tanks, and "Smerch" Multiple Launch Rocket Systems.

DEFENSE POLICIES AND ISSUES

With the new national security concept and military doctrine providing no more than a theoretical framework for policy debate, actual defense policy is driven more by financial constraints than a set of clear policy goals and strategies. While drastic downsizing should release resources over the medium term to create a smaller, more capable, and better-equipped force, Russian strategic planners and their political masters remain confused on all counts. Ultimately, Russia's defense establishment must respond adequately to the radically changed strategic environment and ask fundamental questions concerning the nature and sources of military threats, the types of likely military contingencies, and the identity of potential allies and adversaries.

NUCLEAR POLICY   Until mid-2000, it was widely accepted that nuclear weapons were unique in giving Russia international status and essential for protecting it in a period of conventional military weakness. Russian policy papers reasserted Moscow's resolve to use nuclear weapons first in a conflict to forestall a major military defeat or the loss of a key ally. Defense Ministry procurement policies were heavily slanted toward buying new Topol-M intercontinental ballistic missiles. Subsequently, this view was challenged by those within the General Staff of the Russian Armed Forces who saw nuclear weapons as essentially worthless for preventing and defending against the real challenges Russia was facing along its southern flank. As a result, Topol-M procurements have been scaled down.

DEFENSE BUDGET   The unexpected windfall profits from high oil prices have eased the financial constraints of the Russian government, allowing for more armed forces funding. In the fiscal year 2001 budget, allocations for national defense were increased from R140 billion (US$4.97 billion) to about R220 billion (US$7.8 billion). For the first time since the 1998 financial collapse, funds (R3.9 billion, or US$138 million) were set aside for military reform. In October 2000, the outstanding Defense Ministry debt was transferred to the Russian government's account. In addition, the government promised supplementary funds, if state revenues from oil stayed high.

Yet, it is difficult to know how the money is going to be spent. The transparency of the defense budget has steadily declined and has dropped below even the unsatisfactory standards of the early 1990s. In this climate of unaccountability and abuse, many financial obligations remain unmet. For example, electricity producers have routinely been turning off the electricity supply to military bases, and contract soldiers returning from Chechnya have resorted to picketing military headquarters in an effort to get their pay.

FORCE DEVELOPMENT   The debate about priorities (nuclear or conventional) notwithstanding, Russia is likely to move eventually toward a smaller force size across the board. The SRF will probably be phased out before the middle of the decade, leaving Russia with a tri-service structure. For land forces, heavy tank and mechanized divisions will gradually give way to lighter and more mobile units. The importance of airborne forces is likely to rise, in view of the potential contingencies in Central Asia. Clearly, the air force and the navy will need to emphasize quality over quantity.

Conscription, although much criticized, is likely to continue in view of the high cost of an all-volunteer force and the perceived need for mass mobilization. In fact, for the first time in a decade, Russia practiced in the year 2000 a mobilization exercise calling up reservists in three northwestern provinces.

CONTRIBUTIONS TO GLOBAL AND REGIONAL SECURITY

President Putin's strong position in the Russian parliament allowed ratification in April 2000 of the long-stalled START-2 and the Comprehensive Test Ban Treaty (CTBT). For START-3, Russia has proposed lower levels than agreed in 1997 in Helsinki: 1,500 weapons each for the United States and Russia instead of 2,500. Further progress on strategic nuclear arms control, however, is dependent on whether Russia and the United States are able to reach an agreement on the issue of NMD.

Russia has continued to play the role of a modest facilitator in managing crisis situations. In particular, it sought, with varied results, to help North Korea out of its isolation; to prevent a civil war in Yugoslavia in the wake of an opposition victory in the presidential elections; and to end a new Israeli-Palestinian conflict. On the ground, cooperation with NATO peacekeeping forces in Kosovo and Bosnia-Herzegovina remains generally good. Russia also agreed to participate in a UN peacekeeping effort in Sierra Leone. Conflicts in the former Soviet space, however, remain unresolved. A new mediating effort in Moldova, led by former Prime Minister Yevgeny Primakov, was stalled. Conflict resolution in Abkhazia and South Ossetia was further complicated by the second Chechnya war and deterioration in Russian-Georgian relations. Moscow also cautioned against high expectations regarding its role in Nagorno-Karabakh. The Russian government, however, became more receptive to international efforts to prevent and/or manage conflict in Central Asia, cooperating with the United States, China, and the states in the region.

17 Singapore

THE SECURITY ENVIRONMENT

In the wake of the Asian financial crisis, Singapore showed both resilience and insecurity. Beginning in late 1999, the Singaporean economy restored strong growth, allowing the city-state to shrug off the effects of the crisis. However, the crisis demonstrated Singapore's fundamental vulnerability, and a feeling of insecurity continues to affect the country. The stability of its neighbors, tensions with Malaysia and Indonesia, and doubts as to the viability of the Association of Southeast Asian Nations (ASEAN) as an institution for peaceful cooperation—all these matters are of great concern to Singaporeans.

DOMESTIC   At the turn of the millennium, Singapore, an island with 660 square kilometers of territory and a population of only four million, achieved Asia's highest per capita income outside Japan. Future economic development will emphasize Singapore's status as a center for global finance and the New Economy, specifically information technology (IT), the e-economy, and life sciences.

Politically, the leadership of the People's Action Party (PAP), which has ruled Singapore since 1959, continues. In the 1997 general elections, the PAP won 81 out of 83 seats, regaining two seats from opposition parties and halting its slide in the electoral vote to gain more than 60 percent of votes cast. In contrast to the political upheavals experienced in other Asian countries, the financial crisis did not undermine the legitimacy and authority of the PAP. Rather, most citizens credited the government for steering Singapore successfully through the crisis. In 1999 and 2000, there were some movements toward a freer political system in Singapore, with citizens encouraged to take a more active role in society. However, political changes were at most incremental and cautious.

REGIONAL   Singapore has never faced invasion or threat of war since independence in 1965. Although a dispute with Malaysia over a small islet commanding the eastern channel into the Singapore Strait continues, this dispute has been referred to the International Court of Justice for peaceful resolution. Thus, Singapore confronts no outstanding territorial disputes that threaten warfare. Nonetheless, security remains a preoccupation for Singapore, and some have spoken of a "siege" mentality in the city-state.

Singapore relies on Malaysia for 40 percent–50 percent of its water needs. The island also imports almost all its energy resources and most of its food. Also important is that Singapore is a small multiracial but predominately Chinese society surrounded by considerably larger countries of different ethnicity. Especially, the economic success of the city-state and its status as the regional hub are cause for resentment when narrow views of nationalism arise in neighboring states. As a result of these factors, there is a sense of insecurity that generates a highly realistic outlook among Singaporeans.

Relations with Singapore's most immediate neighbors, Indonesia and Malaysia, experienced controversy and differences during the years of the Asian financial crisis. After 1996, ties with Malaysia deteriorated, following comments by Singapore's Senior Minister Lee Kuan Yew concerning Malaysia's practice of giving preference to the Malays and crime in the Malaysian state of Johor. By 1999, mounting differences divided the two neighbors, including issues such as the continued supply of water from Malaysia to Singapore; the redevelopment of land in Singapore belonging to the Malayan Railway; the right of Malaysians who had worked in Singapore to withdraw their savings from Singapore's Central Provident Fund; and accusations by Malaysian leaders that currency and share speculation in Singapore had undermined Malaysia's economy.

In August 2000, Senior Minister Lee's visit to Kuala Lumpur saw relations with Malaysia improve. Following the visit, exchanges between arts groups and the youth wings of the PAP and the United Malays National Organization developed. Nonetheless, uncertainties remain. In October 2000, Lee commented that the medium-range missiles to be purchased by Singapore from the United States "will face nowhere, but they are there to welcome whoever intends harm." Malaysia's media saw this comment as a provocation, though notably Malaysian leaders did not respond negatively. Efforts to improve Malaysia-Singapore ties are likely. However, depending on the internal dynamics in Singapore and Malaysia, it remains an open question whether the two governments can make progress on outstanding issues.

Singapore's ties with Indonesia fluctuated in 1999–2000. Relations sharply deteriorated after Senior Minister Lee in 1998 remarked that "the market" was uncomfortable with Indonesia's then vice-president, B. J. Habibie. Upon assuming office as president, Habibie clearly resented Singapore, referring to Singapore as a "little red dot" and claiming that it was a country of "real racists." Ties promised to improve when the new Indonesian President Abdurrahman Wahid made Singapore his first overseas visit, reciprocated by Singapore's Prime Minister Goh Chok Tong with a visit to Jakarta and offers of financial assistance. Singapore also joined ASEAN members in supporting Indonesia's unity against separatist movements.

However, after the ASEAN Informal Summit in November 2000, President Wahid lashed out at Singaporean leaders, accusing them of being unsupportive of Indonesia's initiative to include East Timor and Papua New Guinea in ASEAN. Wahid further alleged that Singaporean leaders looked down on Malays and suggested that Indonesia might join with Malaysia to cut off Singapore's water supply. While the foreign ministers of the two countries met soon after Wahid made his comments and played down differences, a degree of unease has enveloped bilateral relations. Singapore's shaky ties to the Wahid government and uncertainties in Indonesia will certainly reinforce Singapore's realist approach to security in 2001.

Beyond Indonesia and Malaysia, ties with other ASEAN members were generally positive, especially those with Thailand and Brunei. ASEAN continues to be a priority for Singapore, and in 1999–2000 the Singapore government was active in promoting ASEAN as an effective means for regional cooperation. At the ASEAN Informal Summit, Prime Minister Goh announced initiatives to assist newer ASEAN members in training. He also proposed "e-ASEAN," a measure to link members through the Internet and other technologies.

MAJOR POWERS   Given its perceptions of vulnerability, Singapore has advocated a balance of power in the region. Singapore maintains close ties with a number of regional and nonregional actors, including Australia, the United States, China, and, increasingly, France.

Singapore views the U.S. presence in Asia Pacific as a cornerstone for regional security. While Singapore maintains no formal alliance with the United States and provides no military bases, military cooperation increased in the 1990s. Singapore hosts a U.S. naval logistics center, provides port and airport facilities for U.S. armed forces, and in 1998 signed a memorandum of understanding for U.S. navy ships to use the Changi Naval Base. The two countries also signed an agreement on administering U.S. forces' access in 2000. By these measures Singapore encourages the U.S. presence in Asia Pacific. Singapore and the United States are also strengthening economic ties. Following the Asia-Pacific Economic Cooperation (APEC) leaders meeting in 2000, Prime Minister Goh and U.S. President Bill Clinton agreed to start negotiations on a free trade agreement. In 2001, Singapore will continue its efforts to engage and keep U.S. interests in the region by reaching out to the new administration in Washington.

Singapore recognizes the need for the regional and international community to engage with China. Because Singapore deliberately constrains defense ties with China to avoid being seen as a "third China," bilateral engagements have been focused on economics. Through 2000, Singapore strongly supported China's early accession to the World Trade Organization (WTO). Although some ASEAN members are concerned about increased competition, Singapore welcomes China's WTO entry and views it as a means to encourage the adoption of international rules and norms in China. In a similar vein, Singapore supports the ASEAN+3 process grouping ASEAN members with China, Japan, and South Korea.

Although Singapore strictly adheres to a one-China policy, it has maintained strong ties with Taiwan since the 1960s. In 2000, Senior Minister Lee visited Taiwan privately and met with the newly elected Taiwanese president, Chen Shui-bian. This led to some speculation that Singapore might again mediate between China and Taiwan. However, this was strongly denied by the Singapore government. Lee said that the visit was only to keep him informed on Taiwan.

DEFENSE POLICIES AND ISSUES

Perceptions of insecurity and a realist outlook force the Singapore government to give highest priority to defending the country's sovereignty and reinforcing the capabilities of the Singapore Armed Forces (SAF).

The city-state's size and population shape its defense force and defense policies. Singapore cannot yield territory if attacked, and defense policies thus focus on brief, decisive encounters. The limits of population size are compensated by compulsory conscription for all male Singaporeans, followed by continued training obligations thereafter. This arrangement allowed the SAF in 1999 to have a total force of 360,000, comprising 20,000 regular personnel, 40,000 national service (full-time) personnel, and 300,000 reservists.

In 2000, the Ministry of Defense issued a blueprint for Singapore's defense policies titled "Defending Singapore in the 21st Century." This publication does not constitute a defense white paper, but rather serves as a confidence-building measure by increasing the transparency of Singapore's defense policies. The blueprint emphasizes two aspects of Singapore's defense: maintaining a credible deterrent by strengthening defense capabilities, and confidence building and cooperation at the bilateral and multilateral levels, especially the development of extensive ties with the defense establishments of regional and global powers.

Another key thrust is to strengthen "total defense." First proposed in 1984, the concept seeks to unite all sectors of society to undertake psychological, social, economic, civil, and military defense. With the end of the cold war the idea of total defense has signified efforts to meet nonconventional threats including terrorism, cyber-attacks, and "new" security issues, such as resource scarcity and the pollution generated by fires in Indonesia. In 2000, the concept also was emphasized because Singapore witnessed increased piracy in the Strait of Malacca. Piracy incidents and terrorism have both been recognized as new security threats that necessitate SAF counteractions.

DEFENSE PRIORITIES AND SPENDING   Singapore voluntarily caps its defense spending at a maximum of 6 percent of gross domestic product. In 2000, defense spending stood at S$7.4 billion (US$4.3 billion at US$1 = S$1.73). This represented 4.48 percent of GDP, well below the self-imposed cap of 6 percent. This still relatively high level of defense expenditure is accepted by the public and strongly supported by the PAP-dominated Parliament.

Singapore's defense spending, however, has led to concern and comments by neighboring states. Since Singapore's economy has experienced rapid and continued growth in past decades, total defense expenditures have increased considerably. For much of the 1990s, Singapore spent approximately as much on defense as did its much larger neighbors. In fact, during the Asian financial crisis Singapore's budget was increased while others in the region cut back.

The SAF recognizes the "Revolution in Military Affairs" and sees this change as an opportunity to make up for Singapore's limited size and population by increasing inputs of advanced technology and training and management skills. In 2000, the Defense Science and Technology Agency (DSTA) was separated from the Ministry of Defense. This move was intended to give the DSTA more flexibility and autonomy in responding to technological advances. The new entity has some 2,400 staff with an additional 900 staff in privatized defense science laboratories. The ministry retains responsibility and oversight. Parliamentary oversight, however, was minimized.

The SAF has also been trying to address Singapore's natural constraints with innovations such as the commercialization of noncombat services (e.g., transport aircraft, cook houses) and more intensive land use by the military (e.g., an underground dump for ammunition). In the future, Singapore's defense policy, shaped by the city-state's continued perception of insecurity, will remain "realist" in its approach. An emphasis on technology and other means to increase defense capabilities should be expected.

WEAPONS PROCUREMENT AND PRODUCTION   Weapons procurement by Singapore attracted attention in 2000. The navy commissioned its first two submarines, conventional Sjoormen-class vessels from Sweden. Two more submarines remain in Sweden for further training until 2003. The navy also contracted for six new frigates to replace aging missile gunboats. The first will be designed and constructed by the French company, Directions des Constructions Navales, while a local company, ST Marine, will build the remaining vessels in Singapore.

Most significantly in 2000, Singapore purchased 50 advanced AIM-120C air-to-air missiles from the United States, worth about US$85 million, with an option for an additional 50 in the future. The air force also began to upgrade its aging A4-SU Super Skyhawks with 20 F16-C/D Fighting Falcons. The replacements will be phased in over the next three to four years.

Singapore's indigenous arms industry continued to expand its production beyond the Landing Ship Tank and Singapore Assault Rifle 21. In 2000, the Bionix infantry-fighting vehicle was launched, the result of a seven-year collaboration between the SAF and ST Kinetics, a government-owned company. This follows the Singapore-made all-terrain tracked carrier, a 16-man multipurpose vehicle.

On the whole, Singapore has emerged as the largest purchaser and producer of arms in Southeast Asia. Arms exports have, however, been confined to fairly basic products when compared to major world producers.

CONTRIBUTIONS TO REGIONAL AND GLOBAL SECURITY

GLOBAL   In 2000, Singapore was elected as a nonpermanent member to the United Nations Security Council for 2001–2002. Singapore's membership will likely bring new dimensions to its international engagements. This effort also marks the culmination of Singapore's increasing commitments in multilateral diplomacy. However, there should be realistic expectations of the influence that a small but strong state can have in world events.

Singapore continued to contribute manpower and equipment to the UN missions in East Timor. Three Landing Ship Tanks, a C-130 aircraft, a medical detachment, and a military liaison team were sent to the International Force in East Timor (INTERFET). In total, some 400 SAF personnel participated. Singapore also contributed a 21-member medical team, 40 civilian police, and three military officers stationed at the headquarters of the UN Transitional Administration in East Timor (UNTAET). To the UN mission in Iraq, Singapore sent four military observers.

In 2000, Singapore implemented its obligations under the 1993 Convention on the Prohibition of the Development, Production, Stockpiling, and Use of Chemical Weapons and on Their Destruction by enacting a Chemical Weapons (Prohibition) Act. This act does not affect present defense capabilities or doctrines because Singapore does not produce or possess chemical weapons.

REGIONAL   The Five Power Defense Arrangements (FPDA) with Australia, Malaysia, New Zealand, and the United Kingdom has been an important element of Singapore's defense architecture since its establishment in 1971. The FPDA treats the defense of Singapore as inseparable from Malaysia's. After some exercises were suspended in 1998 and 1999, the FPDA was back on track in 2000. Defense ministers from the five powers also agreed that the arrangement should evolve from a focus on air defense to combined exercises involving all three services.

During 2000, the SAF also expanded its cooperation in international defense exercises in addition to the FPDA participation. For the first time, the SAF took part in Exercise Cobra Gold at the invitation of the U.S. and Thai armed forces. Held in southern Thailand, the exercise focused on humanitarian aid and peace enforcement, and involved 37 SAF members as planners and observers. The air force participated for the first time in ODAX, a French-led exercise involving North Atlantic Treaty Organization (NATO) countries. Six A4-SU Super Skyhawks and 65 men from the Advanced Jet Training detachment at Cazaux Air Base took part. The air force also joined Canada in Exercise Maple Flag and participated in Exercise Tri-Sling, where F-16, F-5, and A4 SU fighter aircraft trained with their U.S. and Australian counterparts over the South China Sea.

In regional multilateral security, Singapore remains committed to the ASEAN Regional Forum (ARF). Singapore officials support moving the forum from confidence-building measures to the next stage of preventive diplomacy, but they are keenly aware of the hesitation of some countries to do so. In 2000, Singapore also hosted a five-day course for the ARF's Combined Humanitarian Assistance Response Training. The course involved both defense and civilian agencies, with 47 personnel from 17 ARF member countries. Looking toward 2001, ASEAN and the ARF will likely remain a primary focus for Singaporean policy even as the country reaches out to the world and takes on a new role in the United Nations.

18 Thailand

THE SECURITY ENVIRONMENT

Thailand in 2000 continued to experience political and economic challenges. While Thailand's economy has recovered from the 1997–1998 financial crisis, the economic outlook for 2001 is mixed and uncertain. The political and military reforms being implemented have accomplished some successes in battling corruption, improving political participation, and modernizing defense structures. However, the Thai Rak Thai (TRT) Party's landslide victory in the January 6, 2001, general elections make it difficult to predict the political future of Thailand. Externally, while Thailand's relations with its immediate neighbors experienced some difficulties, its overall relations with both the great powers and other neighbors developed smoothly.

INTERNAL ENVIRONMENT *The Economy.* In June 2000, the three-year International Monetary Fund (IMF) support program implemented after the 1997–1998 financial crisis in Thailand was completed early. Thailand's foreign exchange reserves had reached a satisfactory level, and most key economic indicators had improved. In particular, the export sector grew impressively, allowing Thailand to enjoy a massive turnaround in its current account surplus. The economy is estimated to have grown 4 percent–5 percent last year.

Nonetheless, economic problems persist. The banking system is crippled by high nonperforming loans. Recovery is also slowed because the country is suffering from slow regional growth, surging oil prices, and political uncertainty. These factors caused the Thai baht to fall steadily throughout 2000 and cast a shadow over the future.

Many Thais still suffer from the financial crisis. Although the unemployment rate fell from 5.3 percent in mid-1999 to 4.3 percent in mid-2000, 1.42 million people remain without work. The poor have been especially hard hit; surveys indicate a growing gap between rich and poor, and the net income of farmers, who make up more than half the population, has decreased since the crisis.

Some Thai observers are arguing that the country cannot cope successfully with the forces of globalization. Their argument is that pre-crisis high-growth rates were achieved at the cost of the environment and human resources. Therefore, they say, Thailand should adopt a more inward-looking approach to economic development, creating growth as a byproduct of economic behavior that emphasizes productivity, quality of life, and cultural and social values.

Domestic Politics. In the first general election under the 1997 Constitution held on January 6, 2001, the TRT Party won a landslide victory in the House of Representatives. As intended by the Constitution, the election saw the emergence of two dominant parties and the diminished influence of smaller ones. The political outlook, however, is complicated by several factors.

First, forming the new government is likely to be a protracted process. New polls for some 70 constituencies were called in late January 2001 owing to widespread complaints of vote buying and corruption. Second, the political future of the TRT leader, Thaksin Shinawatra, is in doubt. Thailand's new Constitutional Court issued a pending ruling against him for violating asset-disclosure laws. If found guilty, Thaksin would be banned from political office for five years.

The future direction of economic reform under the TRT is uncertain. The party takes a protectionist and nationalistic approach, attacking liberalization policies for allowing foreigners to buy Thai assets cheaply. The TRT has also proposed a national asset-management company to take over the banking system's bad debts, a moratorium on farmers' debts, funding of B1 million (US$23,084 at US$1 = B43.32) for each of Thailand's villages, and a health insurance program for low-income households. These proposals are criticized as fiscally irresponsible. Moreover, the TRT has stated that to implement its economic policies it intends to amend key economic reform legislation passed by the previous government.

Earlier in the year 2000, other elements of Thailand's new Constitution were tested. In March, the country's first Senate election saw an unprecedented high voter turnout and the election of several able candidates. Having real legislative power and legitimacy for the first time, the Senate is set to play an important role in Thai politics.

Besides the empowered Senate, Thailand's three new independent mechanisms, the Election Commission (EC), the National Counter Corruption Commission (NCCC), and the Constitutional Court, performed well. After the Senate election, the EC aggressively disqualified several elected senators because of fraud, requiring by-elections. It took more than four months for the Senate to achieve a full chamber. During 2000, the NCCC embarked on a vigorous fight against entrenched corruption among public officials. In March, the political career of the deputy prime minister, a senior member of the ruling Democratic Party, was ended after the NCCC and the Constitutional Court found him guilty of falsifying asset records.

Confrontational interest-group politics increased. Demonstrations by groups of villagers throughout the country have become more frequent. In several instances, police violently suppressed demonstrators, triggering strong public outcry. Generally, the villagers were protesting the construction of dams and other state-initiated development projects.

CROSS-BORDER ISSUES   With the election of Thaksin as prime minister, Thailand will likely give priority to economic relations. The TRT has pledged to pay more attention to Thailand's immediate neighbors and stick to the policy of nonintervention. The party has also put little emphasis on human rights issues, and border security will remain a principal concern.

Drugs. Drug trafficking is at the top of the foreign policy agenda. In 2000, Army Commander General Surayuth Chulanont asserted that the massive influx of methamphetamines from areas run by the United Wa State Army (UWSA) in Myanmar constituted Thailand's "top external security threat." Military leaders blame Yangon for supporting the UWSA's expansion in areas along the Thai-Myanmar border. Authorities have also found that drug trafficking routes have expanded along Thailand's entire border, with more than 70,000 villages involved. Consequently, border security has been strengthened and various anti-drug measures implemented. These measures include cleanup operations in 117 areas known to be trafficking routes and stiff punishment for corrupt government officials.

Gambling. The proliferation of gambling dens along Thailand's borders with Cambodia, Laos, and Myanmar is a continuing cause of concern among security agencies. In September 2000, tighter regulations

and travel bans were implemented in seven border provinces to prevent
Thai gamblers from crossing the border.

Illegal Workers and Refugees. One year after the August 1999 regulation to restrict foreign labor in Thailand, the government estimated
that more than one million illegal workers, mostly from Myanmar, remained in the country. Private sector pressure led the Thai cabinet to
extend a grace period allowing some 100,000 foreign workers to be
employed in certain types of businesses.

Dealing with foreign labor is increasingly challenging. Foreign
workers do many difficult jobs turned down by Thais, filling gaps in the
labor market. But they tend to be employed illegally, thus facing exploi-
tation and abuse. Law enforcement lacks transparency, with officials
reportedly involved in smuggling illegal immigrants. Also, the problem
has long been tackled on an ad hoc basis. This led the government in August 2000 to establish a permanent organization for managing illegal
foreign labor.

About 110,000 Myanmar refugees live in Thai border camps. Bangkok has consistently called for the world community to pressure Yangon
to take responsibility for these refugees, and in June Yangon agreed to
allow the United Nations High Commissioner for Refugees (UNHCR)
to monitor repatriation. However, the time frame for repatriation was
left to further discussion. Negotiations on repatriation had not begun
by the beginning of 2001, and Yangon continues to attack Bangkok for
playing host to "armed ethnic insurgents."

Transnational Crime. In September 2000, the National Security
Council approved the establishment of a new transnational crime-fight-
ing agency, and in December Thailand signed the United Nations Convention Against Transnational Organized Crime. Security authorities
admit that Thailand has become a base for foreign crime syndicates—
the country is easily accessible, it has become a market for smuggled
arms, and it has loose law enforcement. Several incidents in 2000 highlighted concerns over illegal foreign activities. In January, a group of
anti-Yangon Karen guerrillas seized a provincial hospital and held
more than 100 hostages, and in April it was discovered that Sri Lanka's
Tamil rebels had established a base in Thailand for smuggling ammunition.

RELATIONS WITH NEIGHBORS In 2000, Thailand's relations with
most of its immediate neighbors experienced difficulties, particularly
with Myanmar. As Prime Minister Chuan Leekpai's tenure neared its

end, Myanmar remained the only Association of Southeast Asian Nations (ASEAN) country that he had declined to visit. Chuan made clear that differences with Myanmar could not be tackled on a case-by-case basis but must be resolved in a comprehensive manner. No signs have emerged that Yangon is interested in cooperating on the major issues of drugs, illegal labor, and refugees, making improved bilateral relations unlikely in 2001.

In 2000, Thailand's relations with Laos also experienced strains. In early July, 60 armed attackers clashed with Laotian forces near the Thai-Laotian border opposite Thailand's Ubon Ratchathani Province. Twenty-seven attackers, including 11 Thais, fled to Thailand. Vientiane requested the immediate extradition of the "armed bandits and terrorists." However, Bangkok refused since a bilateral Thai-Laotian agreement on extradition had not come into force. The incident revived long-standing Laotian suspicions of Thai support for anti-Vientiane elements. While insisting that it does not support Laotian insurgents, the Thai government has admitted its inability to totally control the porous border. For its part, Bangkok remains concerned about overseas Laotians entering Thailand to join anti-Vientiane forces in Laos.

On the positive side, during a visit by Prime Minister Chuan to Laos in May, the two countries agreed to cooperate against drug trafficking. In addition, the long-stalled memorandum of understanding on Thailand's purchase of electricity from Laos's Nam Theune II dam was signed. Bangkok committed to making annual payments for electricity of about US$230 million until 2032. In September, the two countries agreed to promote tourism along the Mekong River. Thailand also granted more scholarships for Laotian students to study in Thailand.

Thai-Cambodian relations were also mixed in 2000. Starting in 1999, the Cambodian press accused the Thai military of encroaching on Cambodian territory. In February 2000, the Thai Defense Ministry denied the allegation. However, Cambodian suspicions lingered on, and when Prime Minister Chuan visited Phnom Penh in June, students demonstrated and burned Thai flags. Following these protests, a Thai army unit was ordered in mid-July to withdraw from Kho Tha-ngoc, a disputed hill on the Cambodian border. The Thai army stated that negotiations are needed to decide the future of the area.

Thailand and Cambodia also reached agreement on several other issues. During Prime Minister Chuan's June visit, the two governments signed agreements to jointly survey the border, to combat trafficking in stolen vehicles from Thailand to Cambodia, and to fight cross-border smuggling of artifacts from Cambodia to Thailand. Thailand and Cambodia also agreed to draft a ten-year master plan for economic cooperation, emphasizing the development of border areas. Through this agreement Thailand hopes to diminish the number of illegal Cambodian workers in Thailand, now numbering more than 800,000.

Thai-Vietnam relations entered 2001 on a positive note. For more than half a century, Thailand has considered communist Vietnam an enemy, and, due to suspicions of espionage, adopted a rigid policy toward Vietnamese refugees. However, at the end of 2000 all second- and third-generation Vietnamese refugees were granted Thai citizenship. The secretary-general of the Thai National Security Council stated that the Vietnamese were no longer considered "a significant threat to Thai security." Vietnamese Prime Minister Phan Van Khai welcomed the Thai decision and encouraged Thais of Vietnamese descent to "unite with Thai people to help develop Thailand."

THE MAJOR POWERS   *China.* In July 2000, Thailand and China celebrated 25 years of diplomatic relations. This was highlighted by the first-ever visit of the queen of Thailand to China in October. Chinese leaders praised the visit, stating that both countries had enjoyed "deep feelings of friendship" over the preceding 25 years.

Close cooperation between Thailand and China, forged because of Vietnam's invasion of Cambodia in the 1980s, has flourished and overshadowed differences between the two governments. For Thai leaders, the close relationship stems in part from China's recognition of Thailand's strategic location, size, and abundant resources.

In October 2000, Thailand and China signed a memorandum of understanding on cooperating to control narcotics, psychotropic substances, and precursor chemicals. The memorandum also covers the establishment of rehabilitation facilities and the related problem of HIV/AIDS.

Thailand's leaders occasionally express concern over China's military power, but they do not perceive China as a security threat. During 2000, Thai leaders also grew concerned about China's impending entry into the World Trade Organization (WTO). The major fear is that China might become a formidable competitor for export markets and foreign investment, adversely affecting Thai industries such as electronics and garments as well as agriculture.

The United States. In 2000, the Thai-American security partnership remained strong. Visiting U.S. Secretary of Defense William Cohen proposed in September the creation of "security communities" in the Asia Pacific region, with the objective of enhancing peacekeeping and humanitarian disaster-relief capabilities among regional countries. Although the proposal sparked some concern in the region, it received strong support from Thai leaders, including the army commander. Thai leaders noted agreement between Thailand and the United States on the policy that multilateral peacekeeping operations will be required more frequently in the future.

This view was further reflected in the 2000 Cobra Gold joint military exercise whose format was changed from previous years. For the first time it focused on peacekeeping and peace enforcement and, in addition to 22,500 Thai and American servicemen, also involved the participation of Singapore and observers from Australia, Indonesia, and the Philippines.

DEFENSE POLICIES AND ISSUES

As noted, Thailand's immediate security concerns have in recent years shifted to problems emanating from neighboring countries. The Thai armed forces have played a crucial role in this area, particularly in undertaking operations against illicit drug traffickers. In early 2000, a territorial defense-training program was implemented in 120 villages in eight border provinces. More than 5,000 villagers were trained to protect themselves in the event of armed intrusion. The army plans to expand this program to a total of 592 villages in 2001.

MILITARY COOPERATION   The Thai military is also working with other regional countries to curb illegal activities. In August 2000, the Thai and Vietnamese navies agreed to improve the effectiveness of joint patrols in the Gulf of Thailand. The Thai navy also began negotiations with the Indonesian navy on joint patrols in the Andaman Sea to curb illegal fishing by Thai fishermen.

In November 2000, the Thai army commander hosted the first meeting of Southeast Asian army commanders, though no representatives from Laos and Myanmar attended. The "informal meeting" focused on improving the regional "multilateral security dialogue" and agreed to draft a memorandum of understanding outlining areas of cooperation.

The Thai army commander raised issues such as cooperation on regional relief work and transnational crime.

RESTRUCTURING   The year 2000 marked the beginning of the Ministry of Defense's restructuring plan aimed at modernizing and professionalizing the military. This plan seeks to cut 72,000 positions in the three armed forces by 2007 and to privatize some nonsensitive operations. In addition, in April the army began to phase out conscription and transform itself into an all-volunteer force. Volunteers are now given preference over draftees and receive a range of incentives.

DEFENSE SPENDING   Thailand's defense budget for fiscal year 2001 is B77.2 billion (US$1.78 billion), approximately the same as in fiscal 2000. The budget constitutes 8.5 percent of the national budget and 1.40 percent of the projected gross domestic product. It is the fourth largest allocation after the education, interior, and finance ministries' budgets.

In July 2000, the government approved an air force proposal to buy 16 used F-16A/B Block-15 aircraft and upgrade them to Air Defense Fighter configuration for B5.3 billion (US$122.3 million). This purchase will be funded by the air force's earmarked budget, including a deposit refund of B1 billion (US$23 million) generated by the cancellation of a previous order for F-18 fighters. The air force's F-16 purchase is part of a plan to deploy five air wings of fighter jets. The government stated that this procurement is necessary for national security since neighboring countries have already acquired advanced fighters. However, several observers, including Thai senators, disagreed, suggesting that there was no real national security threat and that more fundamental needs were apparent.

CONTRIBUTIONS TO REGIONAL AND GLOBAL SECURITY

REGIONAL   The government of Thailand believes that ASEAN must stay relevant as the regional environment changes. At the July 2000 ASEAN Ministerial Meeting in Bangkok, Thailand called for ASEAN to focus on human-resource development, spur greater economic integration, and augment existing mechanisms of coordination. Bangkok also successfully initiated several agreements regarding cooperation on human security and transnational crime; the establishment of a ministerial-level ASEAN troika to address potential threats to regional peace and stability; and the development of the Mekong region as a means to help newer members integrate with ASEAN. In May, finance ministers from China, Japan, South Korea, and ASEAN member countries launched the Chiang Mai Initiative, seeking to guard Asia from future financial instability by establishing measures to monitor regional capital inflows and outflows, and to survey and peer-review changing economic conditions.

Since February 2000, about 1,300 Thai personnel have participated in the UN Transitional Administration in East Timor (UNTAET). In July, Lieutenant-General Boonsang Niampradit was appointed head of UNTAET. In addition, Bangkok extended financial and technical assistance to East Timor and invited two East Timorese leaders, Xanana Gusmao and Jose Ramos-Horta, to Bangkok.

GLOBAL SECURITY   Human security and people-centered development lie at the heart of Thailand's foreign policy. Bangkok believes that the world community must create political conditions allowing people to fulfill their basic needs and free them from social and economic threats. To this end, Bangkok hosted a number of international meetings in 2000: the United Nations Conference on Trade and Development (UNCTAD) in February; a ministerial seminar of Asia Pacific countries on "Building Capacities for Fighting Transnational Organized Crime" in March; the annual meeting of the Asian Development Bank in May; and an international congress organized by Thailand, ASEAN, and the UN International Drug Control Program, "In Pursuit of a Drug-Free ASEAN 2015," in October.

Thailand also signed a number of international agreements in 2000. In July, Thailand and India signed the "Utilization of Atomic Energy for Peaceful Purposes" agreement aimed at intensifying bilateral scientific and technological collaboration. In October, Thailand became the fifth Asian country to accede to the Rome Statute of the International Criminal Court, and in December the country became a cooperating partner in the Organization for Security and Cooperation in Europe (OSCE).

19 United States

The year 2000 was a year of transition in U.S. defense policy toward Asia and the West Pacific. As the tenure of President Bill Clinton drew to an end, a number of new regional security issues gained considerable public attention in the United States and within the U.S. government. Dealing with these issues will require significant decisions by the administration of George W. Bush, who takes office in 2001. Some of these decisions will be difficult, because they could affect long-standing U.S. military policies and priorities as well as security relations with key countries of the region, especially China, Indonesia, and Japan.

THE SECURITY ENVIRONMENT

DOMESTIC DEVELOPMENTS   Asia Pacific defense and security policy received greater American attention in 2000 than it had in prior years and involved more issues. China-related military issues were a particular focus of discussion and of partisan differences between the Republican-controlled Congress and the Democratic administration. In June, the Defense Department issued its second congressionally mandated annual report on the military balance in the Taiwan Strait; it concluded that China is enhancing its offensive military capabilities and will be able to launch a massive missile and air attack on Taiwan by 2005. The 1999 report had already spurred the House of Representatives to pass the Taiwan Security Enhancement Act (TSEA) mandating closer administration consultation with Congress over arms sales to Taiwan and requiring the Pentagon to establish direct communication and exchanges with Taiwan's military. The TSEA stalled in the Senate, but in April 2000 the Clinton administration announced a package of weapons for Taiwan that included sophisticated anti-ship missiles and new long-range radar but omitted four Aegis destroyers, which key members of Congress had advocated.

In contrast to the debate over China, the recent domestic debate over U.S. policy toward North Korea was more muted than in recent years. Partly this was due to the dramatic change in North–South Korea relations through the first-ever Korean summit in June 2000. Both the Clinton administration and critics had asserted that South Korea should have the lead role in diplomacy with North Korea, and the general U.S. reaction to the summit was that South Korean President Kim Dae Jung should continue to pursue his "Sunshine Policy." However, concerns began to be expressed in U.S. security and foreign policy circles over the longer-term impact of evolving North-South relations on the status of U.S. troops in South Korea.

Presidential Election. In the American presidential election campaign of 2000, there were generally no major differences between the positions of the Republican candidate Bush and Democratic candidate Al Gore. As in other recent U.S. elections, foreign policy questions were not prominent in a campaign fought mostly on domestic issues, and Asia Pacific issues were only touched on. Neither candidate questioned the need for continued U.S. engagement in Asia. Texas Governor Bush generally took a somewhat stronger position than Vice-President Gore on defense matters such as increasing defense spending and developing missile defenses. Thus Bush's victory is seen by some—including Asian officials—as presaging a harder U.S. line on China and other subjects. As with any new U.S. administration, however, how campaign rhetoric will translate into practical policy decisions will only become clear over time.

The Economy. Increasing signs at the end of 2000 of a slowdown in the record period of U.S. economic growth created uncertainties about the ability of the U.S. market to continue fueling economic recovery and expansion in Asia Pacific. A serious slump seemed unlikely in the short term, but there was general expectation that the U.S. Federal Reserve System and the Bush administration would have to take actions in 2001 to restimulate the economy.

ASIA PACIFIC   *China's Military Buildup.* Reports of a Chinese military buildup opposite Taiwan attracted considerable attention in the United States, especially in Washington, D.C. Concerns were increased by the escalated threat to use military force contained in China's Taiwan policy "white paper" issued in February 2000 prior to the Taiwan presidential election. Two elements of the Chinese buildup create the most concern. The first is increased deployment of ballistic missiles and associated surface-to-air missile installations on China's side of the Taiwan Strait, and increased production of cruise missiles capable of striking Taiwan. The second is China's ongoing acquisition of weaponry (especially missile-carrying destroyers as well as submarines) that could be used against the U.S. Seventh Fleet.

However, many American foreign policy experts, including incoming Secretary of State Colin Powell, warn that an excessive focus on China as a potential enemy would only increase the chances of confrontation. These experts advocate a more measured, balanced approach to U.S.-China relations.

Other Major Powers. U.S.-Japan relations and security cooperation remain very close and generally positive. However, due to Japan's continuing economic doldrums and the relative weakness and short tenures of recent governments, Japan's leaders have limited ability either to deal with sensitive issues in the relationship, such as adjustments in the location of American forces, or to play a leading role in regional issues. U.S-Russian relations, although more directly relevant to other regions of the world, have surmounted the crisis stage generated by the U.S. bombing of Serbia, but they remain troubled by a number of disputes. The U.S.-Indian dialogue continues to expand, with the highlight in 2000 being an exchange of visits between President Clinton and Prime Minister Behari Vajpayee, but fundamental issues of nuclear policy and the India-Pakistan conflict over Jammu and Kashmir remain.

Korea and the U.S. Military Presence. The Korean summit in June, coupled with improved U.S.–North Korean relations (symbolized by Secretary of State Madeleine Albright's visit to Pyongyang) intensified an ongoing debate in South Korea over U.S. troop presence. Kim Dae Jung asserted that at the summit North Korean leader Kim Jong Il had agreed to a continued U.S. military presence in Korea. Reports also suggested that the two leaders had exchanged views on changing the role of U.S. troops to that of peacekeepers. Kim Dae Jung ordered the scaling down of the joint U.S.–South Korean Ulchi Focus Lens military exercise in August following the usual North Korean complaints. He had earlier reconfirmed his decision not to participate with the United States in developing theater missile defense (TMD), and he maintained a noncommittal attitude toward the U.S. national missile defense

(NMD) program. These actions suggested a significant decline at least on Kim's part in concern over a possible North Korean invasion.

The changed atmosphere following the summit also exacerbated preexisting "irritant issues" involving U.S. troops in South Korea. The U.S. military in South Korea found itself under criticism from politicians, the media, and citizen groups over U.S. resistance to negotiate changes in a new Status of Forces Agreement, although a new agreement was finally signed in December 2000. Other issues included the errant bombing of a South Korean village, the dumping of chemicals into the Han River, and allegations that U.S. troops murdered South Korean civilians during the Korean War.

These Korean developments had further ramifications for Okinawa. Okinawan government officials cited the North-South dialogue in hardening their position that there should be a 15-year limit on U.S. use of the new base proposed as a replacement for the U.S. Marine Corps' Futenma Air Station. This appeared to surprise Japanese and U.S. officials, who had believed they had a workable agreement on the Futenma relocation and the support of Okinawa Governor Inamine Keiichi.

Instability in Southeast Asia. The United States in 2000 sought to expand military contacts with Southeast Asian nations, including promotion of military exercises. However, key initiatives were stymied and complicated by political instability in Indonesia and the Philippines that shows no signs of abating. Rapprochement with Vietnam, however, proceeded apace.

The Pentagon took small steps to restore military contacts with the Indonesian National Military (TNI, Tentara Nasional Indonesia), cut off in 1999 in reaction to the TNI's role in atrocities committed by pro-Indonesian militia in East Timor. However, these steps, including a joint naval exercise scheduled for July 2000, ran aground amid new reports of TNI abuses and atrocities in various parts of Indonesia, which suggested inability on the part of the civilian government in Jakarta to control the TNI or to exercise authority outside Java. Indonesia drew renewed international condemnation over the murder in September of three United Nations workers in West Timor by East Timorese militia backed by elements of the TNI. Related criticisms focused on escalated incursions by militia groups from West Timor into East Timor and armed clashes with Australian-led UN peacekeepers. Separatist movements in Aceh on Sumatra and in West Irian on New Guinea and religious strife involving radical Islamic groups also grew markedly in 2000.

The United States and the Philippines began negotiations related to the implementation of a 1999 agreement that provided a new U.S. military support program for the Philippines. The agreement had been motivated largely by Manila's concern over Philippine-China military tensions in the area of the South China Sea claimed by both countries. By mid-2000, Philippine defense priorities had shifted to the escalating fighting with Muslim insurgents in the southern Philippines and the kidnapping of foreigners by the radical Abu Sayaf Group. U.S.-Philippine defense discussions shifted accordingly. Secretary of Defense William Cohen offered U.S. assistance to organize and train Philippine counterterrorism units, and U.S. officials also offered a long-term commitment of U.S. personnel to help train Filipinos in servicing and maintaining military equipment acquired from the United States. However, the severe erosion of public support for President Joseph Estrada and efforts by the Philippine legislature to impeach him at the end of 2000 posed new uncertainties for the nation's politics and policies.

U.S.-Vietnam relations took further major steps toward full normalization in 2000, with the conclusion of a trade agreement and the visit of President Clinton to Vietnam in November. Although the outlook for significant security cooperation (beyond joint operations to recover remains of U.S. servicemen killed in the Vietnam War) remains uncertain, regular U.S.-Vietnam interchange is a positive factor in the regional security picture.

DEFENSE POLICIES AND ISSUES

DOCTRINE   The United States continues to operate under a three-pronged defense doctrine for the West Pacific that was developed by stages from the 1980s through 1995. The first prong is the so-called two war strategy, that is, the capability to fight two major regional wars simultaneously; the most likely locations mentioned by Pentagon officials continue to be the Persian Gulf and Korea. The second prong is to maintain 100,000 military personnel in the West Pacific to assure regional states of a continued U.S. commitment; in practice, this has meant maintenance of the pre-1995 U.S. force structure in Japan and South Korea.

The third prong is the doctrine of "strategic ambiguity" regarding the U.S. role in the defense of Taiwan. The United States takes a non-committal position as to its willingness to intervene militarily should China attack Taiwan. The United States provides arms to Taiwan, but it avoids specifying that any of its forces in the West Pacific have a military mission related to Taiwan. U.S. officials regularly cite only potential missions in a Korean conflict for all components of U.S. forces.

BUDGET   The Clinton administration requested US$305.4 billion for defense programs in fiscal year 2001. The final amount appropriated by Congress was US$309.9 billion, an increase of US$12 billion over the previous year. The defense budget for fiscal 2001 is under 3 percent of U.S. gross domestic product and 15.6 percent of total federal spending. According to Admiral Dennis Blair, commander-in-chief of the U.S. Pacific Command, operations and maintenance expenditures for U.S. Pacific forces in fiscal 2000 were: army (US$659 million); navy (US$5.8 billion); air force (US$1.25 billion); and Marines (US$909 million).

FORCE STRUCTURE   Events in the past year heightened the visibility and immediacy of three issues that will confront the Bush administration. The first is the impact of the changing situation in Korea on the U.S. troop presence in South Korea. Kim Dae Jung's initiatives toward North Korea for a military dialogue and a North-South peace agreement could force changes in U.S. troop levels in South Korea. A mid-2000 report of the U.S. Military Command in Korea contained the first acknowledgment by the U.S. military (except for the Defense Intelligence Agency) of the serious weaknesses of North Korean conventional military forces, including obsolete weapons, major food shortages, and transportation breakdowns. These factors are challenging the U.S. policies of no change in U.S. forces and no negotiations with North Korea over U.S. troops. Statements by Bush advisers Richard Armitage and Paul Wolfowitz suggest that the Bush administration will be more flexible on U.S. troop levels in Korea. Wolfowitz has suggested that a Bush administration would give greater priority to conventional force reduction negotiations with North Korea.

The second issue is the future of U.S. forces on Okinawa. The hardening of the Okinawan demand for a 15-year time limit for the Futenma Air Station and more restrictions on military exercises are increasing pressure for the United States to exhibit greater flexibility on the stationing of U.S. forces. In 2000, some U.S. military officials began to talk about Guam and Australia as alternative sites for stationing and/or training of U.S. West Pacific forces. An October 2000 report on the U.S.-Japan alliance, coauthored by Armitage and former Clinton administration Assistant Secretary of Defense Joseph Nye, called for more flexible regional deployment and training options for the Marines on Okinawa. Thus, prospects are growing for a substantial reduction in the U.S. Marine presence in Okinawa during the next U.S. administration.

The third issue is how the United States should respond militarily to a continued Chinese military buildup opposite Taiwan. This remains largely undiscussed in public because of the strategic ambiguity doctrine, U.S. reluctance to speak of China as a military threat, and the focus of U.S. debate on missile defense systems. Nevertheless, the attention paid to the Chinese buildup in 2000 points to this issue. Analysts within the U.S. military are thinking about it, and the new administration will have to make decisions if the buildup continues.

These issues and the related policy choices have two components. One is the reconsideration of U.S. threat perceptions if China's buildup continues and North Korea's conventional forces continue to decline and/or North-South relations improve fundamentally. The second is the question of whether to restructure U.S. forces away from their Korea orientation to a Taiwan orientation. A restructuring of this kind would entail the commitment of more naval and air forces to the West Pacific, linked to a reduction of U.S. ground forces. The objective would be greater capability to maintain deterrence against China despite China's military buildup and to respond quickly in the event of a Chinese attack on Taiwan. Air force commanders within the U.S. Pacific Command are thinking about creating a rapid response force of heavy bombers, tactical fighters, and supply aircraft that could be deployed quickly in support of Taiwan. In August 2000, the air force moved to Guam 64 cruise missiles that could be fitted on heavy bombers. At the end of October 2000, the U.S. navy announced that it was considering moving three Los Angeles–class nuclear submarines from Pearl Harbor to Guam.

Such a restructuring would necessitate major decisions regarding U.S. forces in Japan and reformulation of the Guidelines for U.S.-Japan Defense Cooperation. Okinawa likely would have to be available for a buildup of U.S. air power. This would be extremely difficult without a substantial withdrawal of Marines to reduce the political problem caused by their presence. Japan could be faced with other burdens, including additional basing of new U.S. naval and air units.

MISSILE DEFENSE President Clinton announced on September 1, 2000, that he would defer a decision on installing an NMD system.

The Bush administration will have to decide whether to proceed and, if so, whether to select the plan favored by the Clinton administration or alternatives. The Clinton-favored plan would involve deploying 20 missile interceptors at an NMD site in Alaska, with the option of later increasing the number of interceptors to 100–200. This system would be designed solely to protect against incoming intercontinental ballistic missiles. The United States would develop the system alone, with no foreign participation. Such a system could be in place after 2005 but likely closer to 2010.

Some NMD supporters, including senior navy leaders, advocate an alternative sea-based NMD system. Missile interceptors would be put aboard the U.S. navy's Aegis ships. Some advocates of the NMD system believe it should aim to intercept an adversary missile early in flight before it leaves the atmosphere. Such a system would require deployment close to the borders of potential adversary nations. However, there is uncertainty over whether alternative systems are technologically feasible and whether the Bush administration will seek to amend the U.S.-Russia Anti-Ballistic Missile (ABM) Treaty before deploying NMD.

The uncertainties regarding TMD are even greater. The United States plans to deploy the Patriot PAC-3 in 2001 and a Navy Area Missile Defense system by 2003. These systems are intended to defend against short-range ballistic and cruise missiles. More sophisticated systems would defend against medium-range missiles. The Navy Theater Wide (NTW) system is the most likely to be deployed after 2007. This system also would be deployed on Aegis ships. NTW tests to date have failed, however, adding doubts to the 2007 timetable. Japan continues to be interested in cooperating with the United States in developing TMD systems, and Japan's Defense Agency announced in 2000 that Japan intends to spend US$280 million over six years to research and develop a prototype NTW system in cooperation with the United States. Taiwan is also clearly interested in such a capability, but provision of sophisticated TMD systems to Taiwan would clearly increase U.S.-China tensions and further escalate the cross-Strait arms race.

The U.S. government cites North Korea's missile program as a principal justification for developing missile defense systems. However, due to the increased attention to the Chinese military buildup opposite Taiwan, U.S. missile defense advocates now increasingly cite China as a justification. If China's buildup continues, China could replace North Korea as the chief justification for NMD and TMD systems.

CONTRIBUTIONS TO REGIONAL AND GLOBAL SECURITY

The major contribution of U.S. West Pacific forces to extraregional and global security is the assignment to the Seventh Fleet of responsibility for naval security in the Indian Ocean, including the approaches to the Persian Gulf. The necessary capability is dependent on naval access through the Indonesian straits connecting the Pacific and Indian oceans. The political deterioration of Indonesia creates uncertainty over the future security of this access.

The future role of the United States in peacekeeping operations in Asia Pacific is also problematic and, as has been true elsewhere in the world, will likely depend on specific cases that arise. In 1999, the United States declined to commit combat units to the East Timor operation but played a supporting role. However, further deterioration of security conditions in Indonesia could revive this issue. The continuation and even escalation of East Timorese militia activity may lead Australia and other countries with peacekeepers in East Timor to postpone plans to withdraw forces in 2001. East Timor's long-term security could thus become a more complex problem. The spread of violence in other parts of Indonesia and the continued inability of the Indonesian government to deal with these situations could lead to other proposals for peacekeeping forces. The United States, Australia, and several European countries discussed openly the idea of international peacekeepers in Indonesia's Molucca Islands when violence between Muslims and Christians worsened in July 2000, and this question may well reemerge.

The United States continues to support and participate in multilateral security forums in Asia Pacific, while still giving first priority to cooperation within the framework of its own network of alliances and other security relationships. One example is the longstanding U.S. effort to encourage trilateral U.S.-Japan-South Korea exercises and consultations, as well as broader "minilateral" dialogues on security issues in Northeast Asia. A related American regional security initiative in 2000 was the conversion of its bilateral military exercises with Southeast Asian countries into multilateral exercises. Singapore participated in the annual U.S.-Thai Cobra Gold exercise. U.S military officials suggested a cautious, step-by-step approach to the multilateralization of the U.S. exercise program, de-emphasizing combat exercises in favor of a focus on anti-piracy patrols, disaster relief, and rescue missions.

The spread of insurgent and terrorist activities by radical Islamic groups in Southeast Asia may increase the interest of regional governments in cooperation against terrorism. Secretary of Defense Cohen's offer to help train Filipino counterterrorist units and Admiral Blair's call for "cooperation between governments" in this area seem to be harbingers of more active U.S. involvement in such efforts in the future.

Some observers speculate that successful U.S. development of NMD might heighten U.S. unilateralist tendencies and reduce U.S. interest in multilateral security forums and cooperation. Unilateralism will undoubtedly remain one theme in U.S. international relations. However, it seems at least equally possible in the short run that development of TMD/NMD capabilities will sufficiently complicate U.S. relations with other states to prompt the United States to intensify its international dialogues and to use all available forums to minimize the danger of destabilizing reactions. But given the technical problems associated with missile defense, any practical impact on the broader U.S. international policy will occur well in the future.

20 Vietnam

The Security Environment

Vietnam enters the 21st century facing both opportunities and challenges. The past 15 years of "doi moi" (renovation) have produced economic growth and a reduction in poverty. However, heavy floods hit the country hard during 2000. The year was also of special significance to the Vietnamese because it marked a number of important milestones. These included the 70th anniversary of the founding of Vietnam's Communist Party, the 55th anniversary of the founding of the Socialist Republic of Vietnam, President Ho Chi Minh's 110th birthday, and 50 years of diplomatic relations with China and the Soviet Union.

INTERNAL During late 2000, the Vietnamese leadership began preparing for the ninth Party Congress scheduled for the first half of 2001. The Congress will assess the implementation of the "doi moi" policy, especially during the period of the past five-year plan (1996–2000). The "doi moi" policy, adopted in 1986, proved critical in promoting economic growth and poverty reduction. Exports and imports soared, while foreign investment and technology transfers began to integrate the domestic economy with the global system. During the 1996–2000 period, economic growth averaged 6.5 percent and exports grew at an average of 18.6 percent annually, topping US$14.3 billion in 2000. During the same period, realized foreign direct investment reached US$10 billion. Foreign invested enterprises in 2000 produced 34 percent of total industrial output, 22 percent of total exports, and 10 percent of gross domestic product.

Although Vietnam's GDP per capita remains low, the country's rankings in the UN Human Development Report increased consistently during the 1990s. According to Vietnamese statistics, the ratio of people living under the poverty line fell from more than 30 percent in 1992 to 11 percent in 2000. For the future, Vietnam plans to focus on education as well as scientific and technological development, especially in the information technology (IT) sector. At the end of 2000, the Vietnamese National Assembly approved reforms to the education and banking systems, adopted a new Insurance Business Law, and amended the Foreign Investment Law.

Despite its achievements, the reform process has also generated problems. These include unemployment and widening income disparities. Income inequalities have been particularly pronounced between urban and rural areas, and have hit ethnic minorities hardest. Moreover, continued rapid economic growth is not yet assured. The economy's international competitiveness remains low, the regulatory system insufficient, and the implementation of administrative reforms slow.

Perhaps Vietnam's greatest challenge during 2000 was the heavy flooding in various parts of the country, which caused massive human and material losses. Despite the severity of the floods, rescue-and-relief operations by the armed forces saved lives and property in the affected areas.

EXTERNAL   Global society, while characterized by an overall trend toward peace and stability, still exhibits many fault lines such as religious and ethnic conflicts. As globalization and the IT revolution affect economies more profoundly, economic security has become a paramount concern. Countries face the challenges of translating globalization into a positive force to eradicate poverty, foster economic growth, and prevent war.

Vietnam's diplomacy is focused on these challenges. In 2000, several breakthroughs helped to promote cooperative relations that support Vietnam's objectives for the new century: to build "an economically strong country with a prosperous people and an equitable, democratic, and advanced society." The leaders of Laos and Vietnam exchanged visits, specifically to discuss measures to manage the two countries' border in the next ten years. Friendly relations between Vietnam and Cambodia also consolidated with the establishment of a joint governmental Commission for Border Affairs to resolve remaining border disputes. The most salient recent events for Vietnam's security were the signing of border treaties with China. On December 30, 1999, a Land Border Treaty settled all outstanding land border disputes and, on December 25, 2000, the two countries finally concluded a treaty on demarcating their sea border in the Gulf of Tonkin.

Sino-Vietnamese relations have improved in other areas as well. Vietnam's Prime Minister Phan Van Khai paid a four-day working visit to China in September 2000 during which the two governments agreed to raise bilateral trade to at least US$2 billion a year. The Vietnamese minister and vice-minister of defense also visited China during 2000, and top Vietnamese and Chinese naval officers met in Hanoi. Finally, Vietnam's President Tran Duc Luong visited China from December 25–29, at which time he concluded the Gulf of Tonkin Treaty and three other agreements.

Dialogues and exchanges at various levels are also strengthening Vietnam-U.S. relations. The most notable events were the meeting between President Tran and U.S. President Bill Clinton at the Millennium Summit in New York in September and Clinton's historic visit to Hanoi in November 2000. These meetings laid the basis for friendly cooperation and regular high-level dialogues on economic matters. Vietnam and the United States have also continued to address unresolved issues created by the war, specifically, the recovery of the remains of U.S. soldiers missing in action and tackling Vietnamese concerns about damages caused by the use of Agent Orange. On the economic front, Vietnam and the United States signed a landmark trade agreement in July 2000. When the agreement comes into force, trade between Vietnam and the United States is expected to double from the present annual level of US$879 million.

During 1999, Vietnam and Japan granted each other most-favored-nation treatment to facilitate investment relations. The already substantial two-way trade between Vietnam and Japan reached more than US$3.7 billion in 2000, and Japan continued to be Vietnam's largest Official Development Assistance (ODA) donor and its fourth biggest investor. During 2000, Japan built two human resource development centers in Hanoi and Ho Chi Minh City, upgraded hospitals, and funded a forestry scheme in central Vietnam. Finally, the two countries held high-level defense and security talks: Vietnam's Foreign Minister Nguyen Dy Nien visited Japan in March and September, and the director-general of Japan's Defense Agency and representatives from the Japan International Cooperation Agency visited Vietnam.

After the signing of an agreement to further promote official state-to-state relations in 1994, Vietnam-Russia relations regained momentum. In September 2000, Prime Minister Phan visited Russia. During this visit, the issue of Vietnam's debt to the former Soviet Union was settled, and agreements on economic and trade relations were signed. However, trade between Vietnam and Russia remains at a low level. During the 1980s, Vietnam conducted 70 percent–80 percent of its trade with the former Soviet Union. Now bilateral trade with Russia only amounts to US$400 million–US$500 million per year, or 3 percent–4 percent of Vietnam's total trade. Russia's President Vladimir Putin is scheduled to visit Vietnam in March 2001, which should further boost economic and political ties between the two countries.

Vietnam's relations with the European Union (EU) have continued their steady development initiated by the signing of the EU-Vietnam Framework Agreement in July 1995. The European Union has become one of Vietnam's most important partners in trade, investment, and development assistance, making it Vietnam's third largest investor and the biggest market for Vietnamese products (excluding crude oil). In addition, the European Union committed more than US$2 billion in ODA to Vietnam between 1995 and 1999, placing it third after Japan and the World Bank.

The Asia Pacific region underwent swift and profound changes in 2000. After more than three years of economic crisis, regional economies are now in the process of rapid recovery, a trend likely to prevail for the near future. Clearly, the most outstanding regional security development in 2000 was the inter-Korean summit. In Vietnam's view, this summit constitutes a significant step toward easing tension and maintaining peace and stability on the Korean peninsula and in Asia Pacific as a whole.

However, Asia Pacific still encompasses potential uncertainties that may adversely affect regional peace and security. Social problems as well as ethnic and religious disputes in several countries are likely to continue or worsen. Therefore, Vietnam believes that ASEAN Regional Forum (ARF) members should proceed steadily by first focusing on confidence-building measures and then preventive diplomacy.

Vietnam also regards the development of a code of conduct (COC) in the South China Sea between ASEAN (Association of Southeast Asian Nations) and China as vital for reaching a durable solution to disputes. At the third meeting of the ASEAN-China Working Group on the COC held in Hanoi in October, the two sides agreed that the code would include fundamental principles, such as the settlement of disputes through peaceful means, nonuse of force, and self-restraint. However, there remain a number of differences requiring further discussion, especially concerning the scope of application of the code.

DEFENSE POLICIES AND ISSUES

DEFENSE POLICY   Vietnam's defense policy remains the same as developed in the 1998 defense white paper. Defense policies emphasize the consolidation of national defense with the People's Armed Forces and public security personnel at its core. Reductions in the size of the armed forces have been carried out and are nearing their final target. Defense priorities are to ensure national security, territorial integrity, and political stability and to enable economic development, reflecting Vietnam's economic, political, military, and diplomatic interests.

Vietnamese military and security experts recognize that to ensure the country's comprehensive security in the 21st century two aspects are central. First, economic development is the most crucial task, because economic security is the most important aspect of national security. Externally, economic security requires expanded economic cooperation while avoiding dependence. Internally, economic development provides a basis for ensuring political and social stability. The second most important aspect of Vietnam's comprehensive security is the military. Despite the end of the cold war, the possibility of conflicts and local wars remains. Therefore, states must continue to allocate a considerable part of their resources to maintain armed forces and modernize military equipment so as to provide a deterrent against external military threats.

DEFENSE ISSUES   Vietnamese policymakers regard the possibility of a third world war as minimal during the next 10–15 years. However, in the early years of the 21st century the world will continue to witness complicated, uncertain, and unpredictable changes. Local wars, armed conflicts, arms races, interventions, subversion, and terrorism as well as socioeconomic crises will persist in various parts of the world. Several security implications follow from this viewpoint.

First, with increasing globalization many Vietnamese see the widening gap between developed and developing countries as not only exacerbating internal social discontent and unrest but also leading to tensions and possible conflicts among countries. Security issues that used to be confined within national territories have now become transnational security concerns.

Second, from Vietnam's perspective, nuclear nonproliferation and disarmament must proceed and the nuclear powers should seriously implement the Nonproliferation Treaty (NPT). Vietnam has signed the Comprehensive Test Ban Treaty (CTBT) and supports the establishment of nuclear-weapons-free zones, such as the Southeast Asian Nuclear-Weapons-Free Zone, to prevent nuclear weapons proliferation. Vietnam also advocates prohibiting the indiscriminate and inhumane use of anti-personnel land mines against innocent civilians, although it shares the view that land mines can be used for necessary and reasonable self-defense.

Finally, the Vietnamese government recognizes a broad range of non-traditional security issues, such as piracy and the trafficking of drugs and humans. It believes that the most pressing of these issues should be identified in order to focus efforts and resources. In Vietnam's view, the alarming growth of the global illicit drug trade and trafficking of small arms are the most grave concerns.

CONTRIBUTIONS TO REGIONAL AND GLOBAL SECURITY

GLOBAL   Vietnam is determined to accelerate the "doi moi" policy and remain a constructive and reliable partner, emphasizing equal cooperation and mutual benefits. Vietnam sees this as a considerable contribution to global security. So far, Vietnam has established diplomatic relations with 170 countries, maintained economic, trade, and investment relations with 167 countries and territories, and become a member of several international and regional organizations.

Vietnam supports the settlement of disputes by peaceful means and seeks to prevent acts of intervention. At the UN Millennium Summit, President Tran proposed using the first decade of a new century to focus global efforts on the reduction of poverty and the elimination of hunger. Vietnam also sees a need to accelerate the reform of the United Nations. The central role of the UN General Assembly should be restored and promoted. Moreover, the UN Security Council's permanent and nonpermanent membership should be increased by including both developing and developed countries, such as India, Japan, and Germany, that contribute considerably to the United Nations.

REGIONAL   Vietnam's active contribution to regional peace and security was acknowledged at the recent 33rd ASEAN Ministerial Meeting, the ASEAN + 3 (China, Japan, and South Korea) Foreign Ministers Meeting, and the seventh ARF. The Hanoi Plan of Action adopted at the sixth ASEAN summit held in Hanoi during December 1998 is regarded as the main guiding direction for cooperation within ASEAN and between ASEAN and its partners. Vietnam has also initiated various projects in ASEAN, including the development of the Mekong subregion, the establishment of a West-East Corridor, and the settlement of pressing social problems such as youth drug addiction.

On the diplomatic front, Vietnam has actively participated in efforts by ASEAN to turn the Treaty of Amity and Cooperation into a code of conduct, not only for relations among Southeast Asian countries but also for their relations with countries outside the region. In addition, Vietnam, together with the Philippines, initiated the ongoing discussions on the code of conduct between ASEAN and China for the South China Sea and signed the treaty establishing the Southeast Asia Nuclear-Weapons-Free Zone.

In July 2000, Vietnam assumed the chair of the ASEAN Standing Committee and the rotating chair of the ARF. Thus, Vietnam now handles on behalf of ASEAN and the ARF matters relating to military-security and external relations, and coordinates ASEAN-U.S. relations. As the chair of the ASEAN Standing Committee, Vietnam exercises a foreign policy that emphasizes the principles of consensus, multilateralism, and diversification. This reflects how Vietnam intends to develop its external relations in the future: with respect for independence and sovereignty; through adherence to the principles of noninterference in the internal affairs of others; with emphasis on equality and mutual benefit; and through a commitment to building regional peace and stability.

List of Abbreviations

ABM   Anti-Ballistic Missile (Treaty)
ACP   African, Caribbean, and Pacific Group of States
ADF   Australian Defense Force
AECF   Asia-Europe Cooperation Framework
AFP   Armed Forces of the Philippines
ANZUS   Australia-New Zealand-United States defense alliance
APEC   Asia-Pacific Economic Cooperation
APMs   antipersonnel land mines
ARF   ASEAN Regional Forum
ARMM   Autonomous Region in Muslim Mindanao (Philippines)
ASDF   Air Self-Defense Force (Japan)
ASEAN   Association of Southeast Asian Nations
ASEAN-ISIS   ASEAN Institutes for International and Strategic Studies
ASG   Abu Sayaf Group
ASEM   Asia-Europe Meeting
BIMP-EAGA   Brunei-Indonesia-Malaysia-Philippines–East ASEAN
     Growth Area
BIMSTEC   Bangladesh-India-Myanmar-Sri Lanka-Thailand Economic
     Cooperation
BIPG   Bougainville Interim Provincial Government (PNG)
BPC   Bougainville People's Congress (PNG)
BRA   Bougainville Revolutionary Army (PNG)
CFSP   Common Foreign and Security Policy
COC   Code of Conduct
CPC   Communist Party of China
CPP   Cambodian People's Party
CSCAP   Council for Security Cooperation in Asia Pacific
CST   Collective Security Treaty
CTBT   Comprehensive Test Ban Treaty
CWC   Chemical Weapons Convention
DND   Department of National Defense (Canada)
DSTA   Defense Science and Technology Agency (Singapore)

EC   Election Commission (Thailand)
EEZ   Exclusive Economic Zone
EU   European Union
FPDA   Five Power Defense Arrangements (Australia, Malaysia, New Zealand, Singapore, and the United Kingdom)
FUNCINPEC   National United Front for an Independent, Neutral, Peaceful and Cooperative Cambodia
GAM   Gerakan Aceh Merdeka (Free Aceh Movement, of Indonesia)
GMS   Greater Mekong Subregion
GSDF   Ground Self-Defense Force (Japan)
IMF   International Monetary Fund
INTERFET   International Force in East Timor
IOR-ARC   Indian Ocean Rim Association for Regional Cooperation
IPSS   Institute of Policy and Strategic Studies (Brunei)
IT   Information Technology
KEDO   Korean Peninsula Energy Development Organization
KOSTRAD   Army Strategic Reserve Command (Indonesia)
LDP   Liberal Democratic Party (Japan)
LP   Liberal Party (Japan)
MILF   Moro Islamic Liberation Front (Philippines)
MNLF   Moro National Liberation Front (Philippines)
MPR   Majelis Permusyawaratan Rakyat (People's Consultative Assembly, of Indonesia)
MSDF   Maritime Self-Defense Force (Japan)
MTDP   Mid-term Defense Program (Japan)
NAFTA   North American Free Trade Agreement
NATO   North Atlantic Treaty Organization
NCCC   National Counter Corruption Commission (Thailand)
NGO   nongovernmental organization
NMD   national missile defense
NORAD   North American Air Defense system (United States–Canada)
NPT   Nonproliferation Treaty
NTW   Navy Theater Wide defense system
NZDF   New Zealand Defense Force
OAS   Organization of American States
ODA   Official Development Assistance
OECD   Organisation for Economic Co-operation and Development
OIC   Organization of the Islamic Conference
OPM   Organisasi Papua Merdeka (Free Papua Movement)

OSCE   Organization for Security and Cooperation in Europe
PAP   People's Action Party (Singapore)
PAS   Party Islam SeMalaysia
PECC   Pacific Economic Cooperation Council
PLA   People's Liberation Army (China)
PNG   Papua New Guinea
PNGDF   Papua New Guinea Defense Force
PNTR   Permanent Normal Trade Relations
PRC   People's Republic of China
RCAF   Royal Cambodian Armed Forces
SAARC   South Asian Association for Regional Cooperation
SACO   Special Action Committee on Okinawa (Japan–United States)
SAF   Singapore Armed Forces
SDF   Self-Defense Forces (Japan)
SOFA   Status of Forces Agreement
SPDC   State Peace and Development Council (Myanmar)
SRF   Strategic Rocket Forces (Russia)
SRP   Sam Rainsy Party (Cambodia)
SSBN   Sub-surface Ballistic Nuclear
START-2   Strategic Arms Reduction Treaty 2 (Russia–United States)
START-3   Strategic Arms Reduction Treaty 3 (Russia–United States)
TCOG   Trilateral Coordination and Oversight Group
TMD   theater missile defense
TNI   Tentara Nasional Indonesia (Indonesian National Military)
TRT   Thai Rak Thai Party
TSEA   Taiwan Security Enhancement Act (United States)
UMNO   United Malays National Organization
UNAMET   United Nations Mission in East Timor
UNAMSIL   UN Armistice Mission in Sierra Leone
UNCTAD   UN Conference on Trade and Development
UNDC   UN Disarmament Commission
UNDOF   UN Disengagement Observer Force (in the Golan Heights)
UNESCO   United Nations Educational, Scientific, and Cultural Organization
UNHCR   UN High Commissioner for Refugees
UNIFIL   UN Interim Force in Lebanon
UNTAET   UN Transitional Administration in East Timor
UWSA   United Wa State Army (Myanmar)
WTO   World Trade Organization

The APSO Project Team

A distinctive feature of the *Asia Pacific Security Outlook* is that it is based on background papers developed by analysts from the region. These analysts, many of them younger specialists, meet at an annual workshop to examine each country paper and discuss the overall regional outlook. They also complete a questionnaire on regional security issues, which is used to develop the regional overview and provide an assessment of changing perceptions over time.

Those involved in the process of developing *Asia Pacific Security Outlook 2001* include the following people. (Note: Paper writers participated in their individual capacities; their views do not necessarily represent those of the institutions with which they are affiliated.)

COUNTRY ANALYSTS
(BACKGROUND PAPER WRITER IDENTIFIED BY AN ASTERISK)

AUSTRALIA   Ross Cottrill, Australian Institute of International Affairs*

BRUNEI DARUSSALAM   Pushpa Thambipillai, University of Brunei Darussalam*

CAMBODIA   Kao Kim Hourn, Cambodian Institute for Cooperation and Peace*

CANADA   Allen G. Sens and Brian L. Job, University of British Columbia*

CHINA   Chu Shulong, China Institute of Contemporary International Relations*

EUROPEAN UNION   Hanns Maull, University of Trier*

INDIA   Dipankar Banerjee, Regional Centre for Strategic Studies, Sri Lanka*

INDONESIA   Rizal Sukma, Centre for Strategic and International Studies, Jakarta*

JAPAN   Katahara Eiichi, Kobe Gakuin University*

REPUBLIC OF KOREA   Chung Oknim, Sejong Institute*

MALAYSIA   Mely Caballero-Anthony, Institute for Strategic and International Studies*

MONGOLIA   Sereeter Galsanjamts, Institute for Strategic Studies*

NEW ZEALAND   David Dickens, Centre for Strategic Studies, Victoria University of Wellington*

PAPUA NEW GUINEA   Ronald J. May, Australian National University*; Lt. Col. James Laki, Papua New Guinea National Research Institute

PHILIPPINES   Raymund Jose Quilop, Institute for Strategic and Development Studies, Philippines*

RUSSIA   Dmitri V. Trenin, Carnegie Moscow Center, Carnegie Endowment for International Peace*

SINGAPORE   Simon S. C. Tay, Singapore Institute of International Affairs*

THAILAND   Julaporn Euarukskul, Thammasat University*

UNITED STATES   Larry A. Niksch, Congressional Research Service, Library of Congress*

VIETNAM   Ha Hong Hai, Institute for International Relations*

OVERVIEW

Charles E. Morrison, President, East-West Center

EDITORS

Richard W. Baker, Director of Studies (2000), East-West Center
Christopher A. McNally, Research Fellow, East-West Center
Charles E. Morrison, President, East-West Center

PROJECT DIRECTORS

Charles E. Morrison, President, East-West Center (United States)
Nishihara Masashi, President, National Defense Academy (Japan)
Jusuf Wanandi, Chairman of the Supervisory Board, Centre for Strategic and International Studies (Indonesia)

STAFF SUPPORT

Hasegawa Megumi, Program Assistant, Japan Center for International Exchange
Kawaguchi Chie, Assistant Editor, Japan Center for International Exchange

Index

Asia Pacific Agenda Project

The Asia Pacific Agenda Project (APAP) was established in November 1995 to enhance policy-oriented intellectual exchange at the nongovernmental level, with special emphasis on independent research institutions in the region. It consists of four interconnected components: (1) the Asia Pacific Agenda Forum, a gathering of leaders of Asia Pacific policy research institutes to explore the future agenda for collaborative research and dialogue activities related to the development of an Asia Pacific community; (2) an Asia Pacific policy research information network utilizing the Internet; (3) annual multilateral joint research projects on pertinent issues of regional and global importance undertaken in collaboration with major research institutions in the region; and (4) collaborative research activities designed to nurture a new generation of Asia Pacific leaders who can participate in international intellectual dialogues. APAP is managed by an international steering committee composed of nine major research institutions in the region. The Japan Center for International Exchange has served as secretariat since APAP's inception.

ASEAN Institutes for Strategic and International Studies

ASEAN-ISIS (Institutes for Strategic and International Studies) is an association of nongovernmental organizations registered with the Association of Southeast Asian Nations. Formed in 1988, its membership comprises the Centre for Strategic and International Studies (CSIS) of Indonesia, the Institute of Strategic and International Studies (ISIS) of Malaysia, the Institute for Strategic and Development Studies (ISDS) of the Philippines, the Singapore Institute of International Affairs (SIIA), and the Institute of Security and International Studies (ISIS) of Thailand. Its purpose is to encourage cooperation and coordination of activities among policy-oriented ASEAN scholars and analysts, and to promote policy-oriented studies of, and exchange of information and viewpoints on, various strategic and international issues affecting Southeast Asia's and ASEAN's peace, security, and well-being.

East-West Center

Established by the United States Congress in 1960 to promote mutual understanding and cooperation among the governments and peoples of the Asia Pacific region, including the United States, the East-West Center seeks to foster the development of an Asia Pacific community through cooperative study, training, and research. Center activities focus on the promotion of shared regional values and the building of regional institutions and arrangements; the promotion of economic growth with equity, stability, and sustainability; and the management and resolution of critical regional as well as common problems.

Japan Center for International Exchange

Founded in 1970, the Japan Center for International Exchange (JCIE) is an independent, nonprofit, and nonpartisan organization dedicated to strengthening Japan's role in international affairs. JCIE believes that Japan faces a major challenge in augmenting its positive contributions to the international community, in keeping with its position as one of the world's largest industrial democracies. Operating in a country where policy making has traditionally been dominated by the government bureaucracy, JCIE has played an important role in broadening debate on Japan's international responsibilities by conducting international and cross-sectional programs of exchange, research, and discussion.

JCIE creates opportunities for informed policy discussions; it does not take policy positions. JCIE programs are carried out with the collaboration and cosponsorship of many organizations. The contacts developed through these working relationships are crucial to JCIE's efforts to increase the number of Japanese from the private sector engaged in meaningful policy research and dialogue with overseas counterparts. JCIE receives no government subsidies; rather, funding comes from private foundation grants, corporate contributions, and contracts.

Five Years of
Asia Pacific Security Outlook on CD-ROM

Asia Pacific Security Outlook 1997–2001
Richard W. Baker, Christopher A. McNally, and
Charles E. Morrison, Editors

This collection on CD-ROM of five years of *Asia Pacific Security Outlook* (APSO) offers readers a new format for reviewing and researching the salient security issues in the region at the closing of the century's last decade. The five original editions of APSO are reproduced in toto, and each of the twenty countries surveyed is newly grouped in five-, three-, two-, or one-year collections (depending on the timing of their inclusion in the series)—for twenty-five books in all. The five-year collection for Malaysia includes the 2000 report on that country, which is not contained in the printed version.

"Live" indexes for the 1999, 2000, and 2001 editions permit instant access to pages cited in index entries in the printed books. A "mega-index" database allows readers to search the complete text of all twenty-five books quickly and easily. The Windows/Macintosh hybrid CD-ROM includes Adobe® Acrobat® Reader™ software for both platforms.

The *Asia Pacific Security Outlook* is a centerpiece of the Asia Pacific Agenda Project, prepared by the ASEAN Institutes for Strategic and International Studies, the East-West Center, and the Japan Center for International Exchange.

Publication Date: November 2001
Price: US$30.00 plus tax and shipping and handling costs
ISBN: 4-88907-057-5

IN NORTH AMERICA AND EUROPE, please order *Asia Pacific Security Outlook 1997–2001* from The Brookings Institution (Fax: 202-797-6004; E-mail: BIBOOKS@brook.edu).

IN JAPAN, please order from Far Eastern Booksellers (Fax: 03-3265-4656; E-mail: sales@kyokuto-bk.co.jp); Japan Center for International Exchange (Fax: 03-3443-7580; E-mail: books@jcie.or.jp); or Kinokuniya Company Ltd. (Fax: 03-3439-0839; E-mail: bkimp@kinokuniya.co.jp).

IN ASIA, please order from The Brookings Institution (Fax: 202-797-6004; E-mail BIBOOKS@brook.edu) or Kinokuniya Company Ltd. (Fax: 03-3439-0839; E-mail: bkimp@kinokuniya.co.jp).